Sherman's Flame and Blame Campaign through Georgia and the Carolinas

… and the Burning of Columbia

Patricia G. McNeely

Pat McNeely

Columbia, S.C.

Sherman's Flame and Blame Campaign
through Georgia and the Carolinas
... and the Burning of Columbia

2nd Edition

Copyright © 2014 Patricia G. McNeely

ISBN: 10-1502595001
ISBN: 13-9781502595003

Printed in the United States of America

United States—History—Civil War, 1861-1865—General William T.
Sherman—Burning of Columbia, S.C. —South Carolina, North Carolina,
Georgia

Cover design by Sharon Kelly and Van Kornegay
Cover image from Harper's Weekly April 8, 1865.
Source: Library of Congress

For additional information or to arrange for book readings or
presentations, contact the author at:

ShermanFlameAndBlame@gmail.com

DEDICATED
TO

Alice Woodson and William A. Gantt Sr.

and

Al, Allison, Alan
Jordan and Julia
McNeely

The South Carolina State House in Columbia was under construction and survived the Civil War. Acrylic painting by Pat McNeely

Columbia's civilians fled to the green at the S.C. College (University of South Carolina) during the Burning of Columbia. Acrylic painting by Pat McNeely

CONTENTS

	Acknowledgments	i
1	THE "WAR AGAINST CIVILIANS"	5
2	EVACUATING ATLANTA	15
3	MARCHING TO THE SEA	23
4	FORTY ACRES AND A MULE	31
5	'A CLOUD OF SMOKE BY DAY, A PILLAR OF FIRE BY NIGHT'	47
6	IS THE TARGET CHARLESTON OR AUGUSTA?	61
7	'THE PANIC WAS REALLY FRIGHTFUL'	71
8	'LEAVING COLUMBIA IN THE HANDS OF THE ENEMY'	79
9	THE DOOMED CITY	91
10	THE THREE-ROCKET SIGNAL	105
11	THE FATE OF COLUMBIA IS SETTLED	117
12	'WE'LL BURN THE VERY STONES OF SOUTH CAROLINA'	127
13	A CITY REDUCED TO ASHES	137
14	WHO BURNED COLUMBIA?	147
15	'HAVING UTTERLY RUINED COLUMBIA'	163
16	ADVANCING INTO NORTH CAROLINA	181
17	PRESIDENT LINCOLN'S LAST WISHES FOR THE SOUTH	187
18	THE END OF THE CAMPAIGN—AND THE WAR	195

ACKNOWLEDGMENTS

I owe everlasting thanks to dozens of friends and colleagues for their assistance and support. I'm singling out two dozen who have spent the most time and effort helping me along the way, but many others have helped in small ways and big. For all of them, I am eternally grateful.

My husband, Al, drove me to dozens of Civil War sites with (almost) no complaining, did some early copyediting and ate a lot of take-out meals, and our children Allison and Alan were always interested and encouraging.

My most heartfelt gratitude goes to Sharon Kelly, who came rushing to the rescue at the end and saved the day—and the book—by spending countless hours helping me cope with never-ending formatting problems. My deepest thanks go to Sharon, who thought I was going to pitch a tent (and almost did) on her front lawn before the book was finished. Sharon also designed the first cover, which was tweaked by Van Kornegay and retweaked by Sharon. I think it's an amazing cover. Van was also an early source of inspiration and let me sit in on a few of his classes at my old digs in the School of Journalism at the University of South Carolina.

Dr. Henry T. Price was another significant life-saver who gave up part of his vacation to do the heavy-duty copyediting.

Henry H."Hank" Schulte did early and late copy reading and was an almost daily source of inspiration and support. His daughter Margaret Schulte was always encouraging and sent "happy spots" to help me along the way.

Doug Fisher was on-call 24 hours a day for my endless questions and spent hours helping me get organized. Early in this venture, my niece Paige Gantt spent hours trying to teach me formatting.

Steve White spent hours hunting for information and leading us on tours through Fairfield County and he always shows up to help.

Bill Rogers and Jen Madden at the S.C. Press Association are a never-ending source of help and inspiration.

Jay Bender and Carmen Maye, who are lawyers and professors at the University of South Carolina, are awesome founts of legal information.

Dr. Ron Farrar read the rough first drafts of the manuscript.

The South Caroliniana staff at the University of South Carolina is amazing. I'm always grateful to Allen Stokes, the retired director, and Henry Fulmer, the current director, as well as Brian Cuthrell, Graham Duncan and Fritz Hamer. Beth Bilderback coordinated the images quickly and efficiently.

Elizabeth Suddeth and Jeffrey Mahala in the Irvin Department of Rare Books and Special Collections in the Ernest F. Hollings Special Collections Library at the University of South Carolina are always significant resources.

Debbie Bloom and the Walker Local History Room at the Richland Library are amazing resources. Anyone interested in history or genealogy should get to know Debbie.

And I must always thank Dr. David Sachsman, who holds the George R. West Chair of Excellence at the University of Tennessee in Chattanooga and is director of the annual Symposium on the 19th Century Press, the Civil War and Free Expression. He and his symposium are always an inspiration.

INTRODUCTION

I keep running into people—especially historians—who believe that Confederates and General Wade Hampton were responsible for burning Columbia, South Carolina, during the Civil War.

Having read an avalanche of eye-witness accounts that leave no doubt that General William T. Sherman's drunken troops burned Columbia, I decided to search for answers. So I traced Sherman's path from Atlanta to Goldsboro, North Carolina, to try to figure out why, in the face of overwhelming evidence to the contrary, Sherman would blame Confederates for burning Columbia and, even more importantly, why so many people still believe that Sherman and his troops didn't do it.

How, I wondered, could so many people think that Sherman entered a surrendered city that had rain-soaked cotton waiting to be hauled away from 100-foot-wide muddy streets and believe that the fires, which erupted on a three-rocket signal at about 8 p.m. on Friday, February 17, 1865, could be caused by Hampton. After all, the Confederate general had been out of the city for nine hours and was camped 20 miles away in Ridgeway when the holocaust began.

I set out to find the answers and help end the controversy that has raged for 150 years. What I found is intriguing and enough to fill a book—this book. I found loose threads of history that you'll find woven together in fascinating patterns of deception that provide interesting new insights into Sherman's campaign through Georgia and the Carolinas.

I've relied almost entirely on primary sources because I've found that some (maybe all) historians, including (gasp) me, have biases and frequently quote from each other. And worse yet, I found some quotes that Sherman never said and some doctored accounts that leave out essential information. As I gathered information for this book, I found that Sherman was his own best source, so I relied heavily on his memoirs, official reports and the accounts of others who were with him or who were unfortunate enough to be in his path at the end of the war.

The biggest loose threads that I picked up were the psychological attacks on civilians and the disinformation and diversion techniques that Sherman developed to, in his own words, "Mystify the Enemy."[1] In addition to his practice (used by both Confederates and Federals) of releasing misleading information intended to confuse and distract the enemy about his direction and military goals, Sherman took every opportunity to blame the nearest Confederate in an effort to cripple the Confederacy by making civilians lose faith in their leaders and their cause.

He was able to fool Confederate generals at every turn with military feints and leaked disinformation; and his strategy of blaming the nearest Confederate for atrocities committed by his men is still persuading some people even today that Hampton burned his own hometown. Sherman said he saw only one drunken soldier the night his troops burned Columbia, and, "I saw no soldier engaged in any act of incendiarism that night," he said.[2] He accused others of atrocities and destruction committed by his men—except for what he ordered or physically witnessed—and he called some of his acts of war "kindnesses," and claimed to have saved what was left.

Strangely, Sherman's brilliant campaign ended in political turmoil with public insinuations from President Andrew Johnson's administration that Confederate President Jefferson Davis had bought his freedom from Sherman. The General who had triumphantly conquered Georgia and the Carolinas was accused at the end of his campaign of being "a common traitor and a public enemy" at the same time his subordinates were being told by high government officials to disobey his orders.

Sherman's campaign through Georgia and the Carolinas was much more complex than just military actions and 62,000 soldiers living off the land. The campaign included a massive psychological strategy to cripple the Confederacy, to destroy the faith of civilians in their leaders and their government, and to kill the will of the people to fight for their cause. Even though Sherman openly admitted most of his strategies and his efforts to "mystify the enemy," those elements have been all but overlooked through the years. However, they were an integral part of his campaign that would help end the war in 1865.

Pat McNeely   August 2014

1 THE 'WAR AGAINST CIVILIANS'

If the people raise a howl against my barbarity and cruelty, I will answer that war is war, and not popularity seeking. If they want peace, they and their relatives must stop the war.

—General William T. Sherman

After Federal forces captured Atlanta on September 1, 1864, General William T. "Uncle Billy" Sherman settled into his headquarters to design a campaign through Georgia and the Carolinas that would become the most brutal and destructive military action ever conducted on American soil.

General William T. Sherman
Source: Library of Congress

Strutting with confidence after significant victories in Tennessee and Georgia, Sherman created a new form of physical, economic and psychological "total warfare" against civilians and private property that he readily admitted would be violent and cruel.[3]

Sherman knew that a war against civilians would be strongly criticized, but he said he had made up his mind to do it "with the absolute certainty of its justness, and that time would sanction its wisdom. I knew that the people of the South would read in this measure two important conclusions: one, that we were in earnest; and the other, if they were sincere in their common and popular clamor 'to die in the last ditch,' that the opportunity would soon come."[4]

He said his campaign would include attacks on citizens and private property,[5] and, "If the people raise a howl against my barbarity and cruelty, I will answer that war is war, and not popularity-seeking. If they want peace, they and their relatives must stop the war."[6]

The centerpiece of his physical and economic warfare was his carefully crafted Special Field Orders No. 120[7] issued on November 9, 1864, that gave his commanders leeway to appoint foraging parties to "appropriate freely" animals, provisions and forage to constantly provide a 10-day supply of provisions for the 62,000-man army and three days of forage. Included was leeway to destroy mills, cotton gins and private property.[8]

General William T. Sherman and his generals, from left to right, James B. McPherson, Henry W. Slocum, Francis Preston Blair, George Henry Thomas, Alpheus S. Williams, Oliver O. Howard, Sherman, John W. Geary, John M. Schofield, Jefferson C. Davis (no relation to Confederate President Jefferson Davis), William Babcock Hazen, Judson Kilpatrick and John A. Logan. Source: Library of Congress

The military orders that Sherman issued in Atlanta and throughout his campaign were so carefully worded that he could and did truthfully deny giving orders for robbing, stealing, destroying and burning personal and private property on the circuitous route from Atlanta to Raleigh; and he could and did, when necessary, blame the nearest Confederates—no matter how far away they were—for atrocities committed by his men.

Therefore, the vast amount of pillaging and destruction that began at full bore as Sherman was leaving Atlanta was not directly ordered by Sherman, but General Orders Number 120 gave his generals wide-ranging authority to organize foraging parties whose voracious pillaging and burning increased in magnitude and ferocity with each passing mile.

Although Sherman and other generals on both sides of the war were not strangers to foraging and harvesting the countryside, civilians and their property were supposed to be left unmolested.

However, Sherman made it clear from the outset that this time was different and that civilians in his path would suffer and private property would be destroyed.

General Ulysses S. Grant
Source: Library of Congress

Although bridges, railroad tracks, arsenals and military equipment, government buildings as well as other buildings that could be used by the enemy, such as foundries, cotton gins and military equipment, were expected and accepted casualties of war, the assault on private property that started in Atlanta frightened, outraged and even terrified civilians, which was exactly the effect that Sherman had planned. He wanted to destroy the will of the people to continue the war.[9]

Even before Sherman left Atlanta on November 15, the Confederacy was making plans for an extensive spring campaign, but its days were numbered. The Western army had been almost annihilated, the important North Carolina posts had fallen, General Robert E. Lee's army was starving, every Southern port was blockaded, and General John Bell Hood had been no match for Sherman in Atlanta.[10]

General Ulysses S. Grant was dug in at City Point, Virginia, coordinating the series of devastating campaigns to be launched by Sherman in Georgia and the Carolinas, General Philip Sheridan in the Shenandoah Valley, and General George Henry Thomas in Tennessee. Grant was also coordinating the siege of Lee's troops at Petersburg that had begun three months before on June 9, 1864, and would finally end nine months later on March 25, 1865.

Grant was attempting to cut off supply lines to Lee, who would be forced to evacuate Petersburg and abandon Richmond on April 2. Lee would retreat to Appomattox Court House, where he would surrender on April 9 and virtually bring the war to an end. Although Sherman was eager to begin his march, he had to wait for the re-election of President Abraham Lincoln and the go-ahead from Grant, commander in chief of the Union army.

After receiving orders from Grant to march to Savannah, Sherman issued Special Field Orders No. 119 on November 8, 1864, in which he served notice that the 14th, 15th, 17th and 20th Corps had been organized into an army for a "long and difficult march."[11]

He ordered wagons to be loaded with nothing but provisions and ammunition and sent all surplus servants, noncombatants and refugees to the rear. None were encouraged to encumber them on the march. "At some future time, we will be able to provide for the poor whites and blacks who seek to escape the bondage under which they are now suffering," Sherman said.[12]

The most significant general orders—No. 120—said that "soldiers must not enter the dwellings of the inhabitants, or commit any trespass, but during a halt or a camp they may be permitted to gather turnips, potatoes, and other vegetables, and to drive in stock of their camp." However, Sherman ordered that regular foraging parties delegated by his officers would gather provisions and forage at a distance from the route being traveled by the main army.[13]

Sherman also issued orders that only corps commanders were entrusted with the power "to destroy mills, houses, cotton-gins, &c., ... and for them this general principle is laid down: In districts and neighborhoods where the army is unmolested no destruction of such property should be permitted, but should guerrillas or bushwhackers molest our march, or should the inhabitants burn bridges, obstruct roads, or otherwise manifest local hostility, then army commanders should order and enforce a devastation more or less relentless according to the measure of such hostility."[14]

Even though the orders clearly prohibited soldiers from entering and burning private houses, the foragers who "ranged at a distance from the road traveled" were a different matter, and—with or without orders from Sherman's subordinate officers—they began the destructive process of robbing, pillaging and burning private property while providing Sherman with official deniability of atrocities against the civilian population. He said he would not believe any oath of any one who saw a fire kindled by his men in a house or shed. "I would not believe it, unless it were confirmed by some of my own people," he said.[15] When confronted in later years about some of the destruction described by witnesses in South Carolina, he said, "Well, they would have to state the names of the officers, and if the officers denied it, I would accept their denial rather than any evidence of people in South Carolina."[16]

Sherman knew how to keep his own hands clean and would sanctimoniously describe "the only act of vandalism that I recall done by myself personally during the war" was a bitter cold night in Pocotaligo, South Carolina, when he burned an "old mantel clock and the wreck of a bedstead" to stay warm.[17]

Each of his 40 brigades was permitted to have 50 foragers, which meant 2,000 men would leave on foot to roam over the countryside to confiscate supplies and livestock. Although some soldiers foraged close by the marching army, the "bummers," as they would soon be called by victims in their path, were encouraged to circulate freely for up to 30 miles or more in front and on either side of the army line over an average breadth of 40 miles while others lagged behind destroying railroads.[18]

After confiscating everything of value and destroying most of what was left, the triumphant foragers would meet their brigades along the march driving mules hauling wagon loads of hams, poultry, vegetables and forage corn and herding cattle, hogs, sheep, and as Sherman would claim later, as many as 2,000 new horses a day.[19]

As the foragers returned, guards were usually posted with stolen property until the proper wagons came along. However, the wagons were not allowed to halt and had to be loaded with the confiscated goods as they passed.[20] The rear guard was charged with destroying railroad lines by twisting the rails into Sherman's Bowties, or Neckties, mounds of iron that could not be used again.[21]

Although his foraging strategy made his army look ragged, scattered and disorganized, Sherman was able to accomplish his single-minded mission to cripple the Confederacy because his men were so perfectly disciplined that he could conduct precision strikes.

Although Sherman's officers, including General Oliver Howard, issued orders along the way in an effort to stop the wanton destruction that began in Atlanta, the foragers stopped only when the order came directly from Sherman.[22] Sherman showed evidence that he could reduce the level of destruction at any time, as he did in Milledgeville[23] or, even more significantly, stop the destruction, as he did in Savannah, which he protected because Grant had other plans for the city after Sherman's departure.

Sherman pointed out the exemplary behavior of his troops in Savannah, "so manly, so quiet, so perfect, that I take it as the best evidence of discipline and true courage."[24] Yet his reports about his troops who robbed and burned the surrendered city of Columbia were brief and defensive with no praise for their "manly" and "perfect" discipline.

Although Sherman was quite aware of the vast extent of pillaging and destruction, he always protected his men and permitted the destruction to continue.

Sherman would coyly admit in his official report after the war that his army had been "a little loose in foraging.... They 'did some things they ought not to have done,' yet on the whole they have supplied the wants of the army with as little violence as could be expected and with as little loss as I calculated."[25]

And when his foragers got a "little loose in foraging," he simply "mystified the enemy," as he would call it, by blaming Confederates— even if they were miles away.[26] The policy would prove to be so effective that by the time Sherman reached Savannah, he would estimate the damage to the state of Georgia and its military resources at $100 million (more than $1.4 billion in 2014 dollars),[27] of which at least $20 million (more than $280 million in 2014 dollars) was in confiscated property, "waste and destruction."[28]

A part of his propaganda and "mystification" plan already in place when he entered Atlanta included controlling the media as much as possible. Sherman believed that war correspondents were "spies and defamers with the impudence of Satan." He wrote, "In giving intelligence to the enemy in sowing discord and discontent in an army, these men fulfill all the conditions of spies and have brought our country to the brink of ruin." Sherman, who made no secret of his hatred for newspaper correspondents, was like most generals—both Federal and Confederate—who allowed in his army only those reporters who met his stringent conditions of controlled news. "For my part though silent, I have at times felt that I would prefer to be governed by Davis, Beauregard & Bragg, [than] to be thus abused by a set of dirty newspaper scribblers who have the impudence of Satan," he said. "They come into camp, poke around among the lazy shirks & pick up their camp Rumors & publish them as facts ... . They are a pest and Shall not approach me, and I will treat them as spies, which in truth they are."[29]

Sherman's troops destroyed every railroad they could find during the campaign through Georgia and the Carolinas. *Source: Library of Congress*

Sherman's dislike and distrust of the press stemmed from the period from November 9, 1861, to February 14, 1862, when he possibly had a nervous breakdown and had been removed from his command.[30] He had gone on leave under a cloud of uncertainty, with his sanity being questioned in the newspapers, and although he returned to active duty three months later in command of the District of Cairo, he would never forgive the press.[31]

Even though Sherman disliked—even hated—the press, he allowed embedded war correspondents and illustrators in his army, but reporters were so tightly censored and controlled that any who displeased generals, in both Federal and Confederate armies, were ejected from the camps without access to any official information, which was normally a career-ending move for a war correspondent. The reporters were actually in the army, usually at officer rank but without any military duties, and they were paid by their newspapers but did not draw Army pay. They also had to provide their own horses, forage and food, and in many cases were not allowed to buy food and forage from the army. By the middle of the war, the reporters were also dependent on the military telegraph, which was

Increasing numbers of freedmen, refugees and sympathizers followed Sherman's troops during his campaign through Georgia and the Carolinas.
Source: Library of Congress

heavily censored, unless they used the mail, which was slow and unreliable.[32]

Sherman's order also provided that able-bodied slaves could be taken along at the discretion of each army commander.[33] Although Sherman specified "able bodied," he would acquire thousands of former slaves—including old men, women and children—who would become an increasing burden as the troops marched toward Savannah. Knowing that Sherman only wanted able-bodied freedmen, the soldiers had their own way of getting rid of unwanted slaves. "The d___d negroes, as a rule, prefer to stay at home, particularly after they found out that we only wanted able bodied men (and to tell you the truth, the youngest and best looking women)," according to Lieutenant Thomas Myers of Boston. "Sometimes we take off whole families and plantations of negroes by way of repaying the secessionists, but the useless part of these we soon manage to lose— sometimes in crossing rivers—sometimes in other ways."[34]

Even though the troops were managing to "lose" some of the slaves, their numbers had grown into the thousands by time Sherman reached Savannah. Feeding and sheltering the freedmen straggling along behind the Federal troops was becoming a major problem, but, of equal interest to the Lincoln Administration, Sherman was perceived as having made no effort to incorporate the able-bodied slaves into the army. The freedmen would become a national political problem for Sherman by the time he reached Savannah.

In addition to almost never taking personal official responsibility for any destruction in his path, Sherman established rules concerning property: "severe but just—founded upon the laws of nations and the practice of civilized governments and am clearly of the opinion that we should claim all the belligerent rights over conquered countries, that the people may realize the truth that war is no child's play."[35]

To that end, he believed that all Confederate property, both public and private, belonged to the federal government and therefore was his to confiscate, destroy and in some cases to redistribute. He occasionally gave away some of the confiscated livestock and other goods and supplies, as he did in Savannah and Columbia, but in his most significant reallocation of Confederate property, he gave freedmen all the property 30 miles inland from Charleston to Jacksonville, Florida, in an effort to relocate the emancipated slaves who were following his army.

Sherman carefully protected himself and the Federal government against claims such as those made by England and citizens after the war against the Federal government for lost property under regulations of the Mixed Commission on British and American Claims.[36]

To that end, Sherman told the commanders in his special orders that foragers could not give receipts for lost or confiscated property but could give written certificates of the facts, if they chose.

However, apparently no one in his army chose to do either, and when the hearings on lost property claims were held between 1871 and 1873, apparently no one in South Carolina produced any signed documents proving that Federal soldiers had confiscated or destroyed property.[37]

In line with Sherman's protection of claims against the government, Secretary of War Edwin M. Stanton, who was a lawyer, ordered the obliteration of all marks of identification on bales of confiscated cotton to reduce the claims

Secretary of War Edwin M. Stanton. Source: Library of Congress

against the U.S. Treasury after the war. Sherman would later say that claims were made for three times the amount of cotton actually captured and that reclamations on the Treasury "have been allowed for more than the actual quantity captured," which he claimed was "only 31,000 bales."[38]

However, Sherman was "mystifying the record" since he had shipped 25,000 bales to Lincoln along with his Christmas message and was not claiming credit for thousands of other bales captured and shipped out of the South after his departure. Nor was he taking credit for cotton his troops burned but that he usually blamed on Confederates or "stragglers" in his march through Georgia and the Carolinas.[39]

2 EVACUATING ATLANTA

War is cruelty, and you cannot refine it; and those who brought war into our country deserve all the curses and maledictions a people can pour out.

—William T. Sherman

Sherman's idea to wage war against the civilian population crystalized almost immediately after the capture of Atlanta when he decided that military occupation of numerous southern cities was crippling the army.

He concluded that conquered cities should be destroyed

General John Bell Hood
Source: Library of Congress

instead of occupied with a Federal force. He had seen Memphis, Vicksburg, Natchez, and New Orleans all captured from the enemy, and each at once garrisoned by a full division of troops, if not more; so he concluded that success was actually crippling Federal armies in the field by forcing them to leave detachments to guard and protect the interests of a hostile population.

He resolved to make Atlanta a temporary military garrison or depot, with no civilian population to influence military measures, but he was planning to burn the city on his departure.[40] In a letter to Confederate General John Bell Hood dated September 7, Sherman said that he had ordered all the citizens in Atlanta to evacuate the city—either north or south. He proposed a two-day truce to move the citizens out of the city. He said he could provide food and transportation to any residents who wanted to go to Tennessee,

Kentucky or farther north, and he would take the remaining residents to Rough and Ready, a small town near Atlanta.[41]

Hood protested Sherman's proposed evacuation of the citizens of Atlanta saying, "And now, sir, permit me to say that the unprecedented measure you propose transcends, in studied and ingenious cruelty, all acts ever before brought to my attention in the dark history of war. In the name of God and humanity, I protest, believing that you will find that you are expelling from their homes and firesides the wives and children of a brave people."[42]

Sherman denied that his actions were unprecedented and retaliated by accusing General Joseph "Fightin' Joe" Johnston of moving families from Dalton to Atlanta, "and I see no reason why Atlanta should be excepted," Sherman said as justification. "You yourself burned dwelling-houses along your parapet, and I have seen today fifty houses that you have rendered uninhabitable because they stood in the way of your forts and men. You defended Atlanta on a line so close to town that every cannon-shot and many musket-shots from our line of investment, that overshot their mark, went into the habitations of women and children."[43]

Sherman also blamed General William J. Hardee for taking similar actions at Jonesboro, Georgia, and Johnston of the same at Jackson, Mississippi. "I have not accused you of heartless cruelty, but merely instance these cases of very recent occurrence, and could go on and enumerate hundreds of others, and challenge any fair man to judge which of us has the heart of pity for the families of a 'brave people.'" Sherman said.[44]

Hood denied all of Sherman's accusations, saying that Johnston "depopulated no villages, nor towns, nor cities, either friendly or hostile" in Dalton, Georgia, nor did he and Hardee expel anyone from Atlanta.

As accusations flew back and forth, Sherman's blame list grew longer as he railed at Hood: "In the name of common-sense, I ask you not to appeal to a just God in such a sacrilegious manner. You who, in the midst of peace and prosperity, have plunged a nation into war—dark and cruel war— who dared and badgered us to battle, insulted our flag, seized our arsenals and forts that were left in the honorable custody of peaceful ordnance-sergeants, seized and made 'prisoners

Citizens gather at the Provost Marshal's Office in Atlanta to get passes to go "north and south" after Sherman ordered the evacuation of the city.
Source: Library of Congress

of war' the very garrisons sent to protect your people against negroes and Indians, long before any overt act was committed by the (to you) hated Lincoln Government; tried to force Kentucky and Missouri into rebellion, spite of themselves; falsified the vote of Louisiana; turned loose your privateers to plunder unarmed ships; expelled Union families by the thousands, burned their houses, and declared, by an act of your Congress, the confiscation of all debts due Northern men for goods had and received! Talk thus to the marines, but not to me, who have seen these things, and who will this day make as much sacrifice for the peace and honor of the South as the best-born Southerner among you! If we must be enemies, let us be men, and fight it out as we propose to do, and not deal in arch hypocritical appeals to God and humanity."[45]

Hood was even angrier with Sherman's response. "I see nothing in your communication which induces me to modify the language of condemnation with which I characterized your order. It but strengthens me in the opinion that it stands 'preeminent in the dark history of war for studied and ingenious cruelty.'"

Hood berated Sherman for shelling Atlanta without notice, a warning that he said is "usual in war among civilized nations."[46] In response to Hood, Sherman wrote, "I was not bound by the laws of war to give notice of the shelling of Atlanta, a 'fortified town, with magazines, arsenals, foundries and public stores;' you were bound to take notice. See the books."[47] Sherman flipped 180 degrees on February 15 when his troops reached the west bank of the Congaree outside Columbia and Confederates shelled the camp at night without warning. Angrily, he said, "This provoked me much at the time, for it was wanton mischief.... I have always contended that I would have been justified in retaliating for this unnecessary act of war, but did not, though I always characterized it as it deserved."[48]

Sherman described his order to evacuate the citizens of Atlanta as an "act of kindness to these families." It was typical of the disinformation and propaganda that he would disseminate in his new "total war" culture, and he became increasingly adept at "mystifying the enemy" by spinning his acts of war—usually his most barbaric—into "kindnesses."[49]

While Sherman was still in Atlanta, Hood's letter was followed on September 11 by a plea from Atlanta Mayor James M. Calhoun and

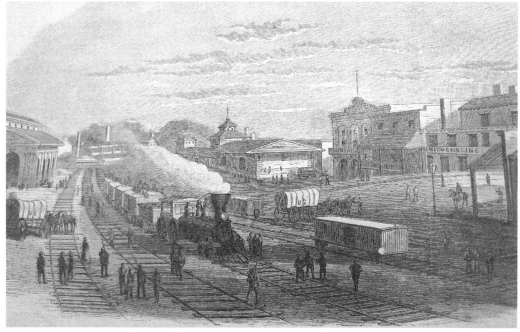

After evacuating Atlanta, Sherman settled in to plan the campaign through Georgia and the Carolinas. Source: Library of Congress

two councilmen, who described the "heart-breaking condition" of many of the women and children in Atlanta who were to be transported into the woods of north Georgia in the middle of the winter.

"We know of no instance ever having occurred—surely never in the United States—and what has this helpless people done, that they should be driven from their homes, to wander strangers and outcasts, and exiles, and to subsist on charity?" The mayor begged Sherman to reconsider his order and "suffer this unfortunate people to remain at home, and enjoy what little means they have."[50]

Sherman denied the mayor's plea, saying, "I cannot discuss this subject with you fairly because I cannot impart what we propose to do, but I assert that our military plans make it necessary for the inhabitants to go away, and I can only renew my offer of services to make their exodus in any direction as easy and comfortable as possible."[51]

He assured the mayor: "You cannot qualify war in harsher terms than I will. War is cruelty, and you cannot refine it; and those who brought war into our country deserve all the curses and maledictions a people can pour out."[52]

After a long discussion in his letter about the horrors of war, Sherman said, "You might as well appeal against the thunder-storm as against these terrible hardships for the campaign through Georgia. They are inevitable, and the only way the people of Atlanta can hope once more to live in peace and quiet at home, is to stop the war, which can only be done by admitting that it began in error and is perpetuated in pride."[53]

Sherman ended by ordering the Mayor to execute his order. "Now you must go, and take with you the old and feeble, feed and nurse them, and build for them, in more quiet places, proper habitations to shield them against the weather until the mad passions of men cool down, and allow the Union and peace once more to settle over your old homes in Atlanta."[54]

Outraged, Hood wrote to Sherman on September 12: "You order into exile the whole population of a city; drive men, women and children from their homes at the point of the bayonet, under the plea that it is to the interest of your Government, and on the claim that it is 'an act of kindness to these families of Atlanta.' ...You issue a sweeping edict covering all the inhabitants of a city, and add insult to injury heapcd upon the defenseless by assuming that you have done them a kindness."[55]

However, the issue was settled. The evacuation was part of Sherman's "total war" strategy from which he would not waver. He had issued his terms of evacuation, and in spite of the protestations of Hood and the mayor of Atlanta, the entire civilian population was gone by the middle of September, exactly as Sherman had ordered.

In addition to the psychological terror caused by the evacuation and burning of Atlanta, Sherman wanted to avoid leaving troops in the city when he left, a situation that he explained in a letter to Grant's Chief of Staff General Henry Halleck on September 20.

Sherman said he had evacuated all citizens from Atlanta because he wanted all the houses for military storage and occupation and he wanted to contract the lines of defense to diminish the garrison to the narrow and vital parts instead of embracing the suburbs.

"Atlanta is a fortified town, was stubbornly defended, and fairly captured," he wrote. "As captors, we have a right to it."[56] He said a civilian population calls for provost guards and absorbs the attention of officers "in listening to everlasting complaints and special grievances that are not military."[57]

His action to evacuate the civilian population from Atlanta was approved after the fact by the U.S. War Department. Halleck wrote on September 28, "Not only are you justified by the laws and usages of war in removing these people, but I think it was your duty to your own army to do so."

He also said Sherman would be justified in foraging for provisions both in Atlanta and "in your march farther into the enemy's country.... Let the disloyal families of the country, thus stripped, go to their husbands, fathers, and natural protectors, in the rebel ranks; we have tried three years of conciliation and kindness without any reciprocation; on the contrary, those thus treated have acted as spies and guerrillas in our rear and within our lines."[58]

Sherman was so intent on maintaining the strength of his own army while reducing the size and strength of the Confederate armies before leaving Atlanta that he refused to exchange prisoners with Hood. Sherman sent 2,000 prisoners back to Hood to exchange with other Federal officers because, Sherman said, "I would not exchange for his prisoners generally, because I knew these would have to be sent to their own regiments, away from my army, whereas all we could give him could at once be put to duty in his immediate army."[59]

Sherman settled down with his army in Atlanta to wait for the November election. The telegraph and railroads had been repaired, and Sherman had uninterrupted communication to the rear. Trains arrived with regularity bringing ample supplies.

As Sherman studied his next move, he was convinced more than ever that he should pursue the route to the sea. In a letter written on September 20, to Grant, who had been holed up since June at City Point, Virginia, watching over the siege of Petersburg, Sherman said, "I admire your dogged perseverance and pluck more than ever. If you can whip Lee and I can march to the Atlantic, I think Uncle Abe will give us a twenty days' leave of absence to see the young folks."[60]

When two friends of Georgia Governor Joseph E. Brown dropped by in search of the body of a Confederate who had been killed near Cassville (near Atlanta), Sherman took the opportunity to send a warning. "I told him, if he saw Governor Brown, to describe to him fully what he had seen, and to say that if he remained inert, I would be compelled to go ahead, devastating the State in its whole length and breadth; that there was no adequate force to stop us, etc.; but if he would issue his proclamation withdrawing his State troops from the armies of the Confederacy, I would spare the State, and in our passage across it confine the troops to the main roads, and would, moreover, pay for all the corn and food we needed."[61]

The governor immediately notified Hood that he was withdrawing the Georgia militia from his command, but instead of full withdrawal from the Confederacy, the governor dispersed them to their homes "to gather the corn and sorghum, then ripe and ready for the harvesters."[62] That was not good enough for Sherman, who accused the governor of simply giving a furlough to the militia and calling for a special session of the Legislature at Milledgeville to consider the critical condition of affairs in the state.[63]

The governor's failure to comply meant that Sherman had an excuse for not confining his troops to the main roads and for not paying for anything that would be confiscated by the foragers, and more importantly, he could blame the governor—the nearest Confederate—for all the burning and pillaging that was about to occur in Georgia.

In the next month after the fall of Atlanta, skirmishing continued in Sherman's backyard in Georgia while President Lincoln campaigned for re-election against George B. McClellan, a Democrat running as the "peace candidate." Lincoln was still anxious about the election, but the victories in Atlanta and the Shenandoah had helped his cause.[64] With increasing anxiety, President Jefferson Davis headed for Macon, Georgia, on September 20 to see what could be done to reverse the rapidly declining fortunes of the Confederate cause.[65]

Confederate President Jefferson Davis
Source: Library of Congress

Hood was in northwest Georgia still smarting from his defeat in the Battle of Atlanta and Confederate losses in Tennessee. However, since he was still hunting for a chink in Sherman's armor, he attacked along the Chattanooga-Atlanta railroad, skirmishing toward Chattanooga in what Sherman correctly perceived as an effort to lure him back toward Tennessee.[66]

3 MARCHING TO THE SEA

I can make this march and make Georgia howl.

—*William T. Sherman*

Sensing that the time was right, Sherman urgently telegraphed Grant on October 10 asking for approval to strike out with wagons for Milledgeville, Millen and Savannah. "I can make this march, and make Georgia howl! " he wrote. "We have on hand over eight thousand head of cattle and three million rations of bread, but no corn. We can find plenty of forage in the interior of the State."[67] He telegraphed again the same day, saying, "I can make Savannah, Charleston, or the mouth of the Chattahoochee (Appalachicola). Answer quick, as I know we will not have the telegraph long."[68]

General Joseph Wheeler
Source: Library of Congress

Although Sherman continued to send forces a few miles outside Atlanta to skirmish with Confederate forces, Hood's efforts to lure Sherman back toward Tennessee and Alabama had failed. When Hood turned the Army of Tennessee toward Alabama on October 17, only a small force of 2,000 Confederate cavalry under General Joseph "Fightin' Joe" Wheeler had been left to skirmish with Sherman.[69] Hood's absence opened a door straight through Georgia to the sea at a time that Sherman considered the perfect moment to abandon his Federal supply lines and live off the land.[70] He had studied census records to determine the best route to provide food and supplies for his army and forage for the animals.

President Lincoln wanted Sherman to hold off on entering enemy territory until after the presidential election on November 8, but, sensing victory in the election, Grant sent word on November 2 that he approved of the march to the sea instead of overland to join him in Virginia. Sherman telegraphed Grant that he was planning to march on November 10, as soon as the election was over.

As part of his preparation, Sherman ordered General John M. Corse to burn all the mills, factories and everything useful to the enemy in middle Georgia in case Confederates should decide to pursue or resume military possession of the area.

Sherman's troops at work leveling and setting fire to the great depot, round house and other parts of Atlanta. The heart of the city was in flames all through the night. Source: Library of Congress

Convinced that the greater part of General P.G.T. Beauregard's army was in Alabama, Sherman issued orders on November 12 for all detachments to march rapidly back to Atlanta, breaking up the railroad en route "generally to so damage the country as to make it untenable to the enemy."[71] By November 14, all troops had gathered in and around Atlanta. All railroad and telegraph communications with the rear were broken.

"The army stood detached from all friends, dependent on its own resources and supplies," Sherman wrote. "No time was to be lost."[72]

So that it would not be necessary to leave an occupying force, Sherman had decided that he would not garrison Atlanta or any other cities on his route to the sea and on to North Carolina, even though he only had orders at that time to go as far as Savannah. Since he had decided to destroy rather than occupy most cities and towns and little cross-roads in his path, Federal forces were at work by November 14 leveling and setting fire to the great depot, round house and machine shops of the Georgia railroad and other parts of Atlanta. The fire came close to Judge Richard F. Lyon's house where Sherman was quartered, and soon reached the block of stores near the depot. The heart of the city was in flames all night.[73]

Sherman divided his army of 62,204 men into two equal wings, the right wing containing the 15th and 17th Corps commanded by General Oliver Howard, and the left wing, containing the 14th and the 20th Corps, commanded by General Henry W. Slocum. General Judson Kilpatrick led the cavalry.[74]

The number of guns had been reduced to 65, or about one gun to each thousand men, and they were generally in batteries of four guns each. Each wagon loaded with gun, caisson and forges was drawn by four teams of horses. "We had in all about 2,500 wagons, with teams of six mules to each, and 600 ambulances," Sherman said. "Each soldier carried on his person 40 rounds of ammunition, and in the wagons were enough cartridges to make up about two rounds per man, and in like manner 200 rounds of assorted ammunition were carried for each gun."[75]

General P.G.T. Beauregard
Courtesy of South Caroliniana Library at the University of South Carolina, Columbia, S.C. Columbia, S.C.

Sherman reported that the troops had 1.2 million rations, which was about 20 days supply, with a good supply of beef cattle to be driven along on the hoof.[76] He had estimated that each soldier would need "about three gross of food per day, and the horse or mule about twenty pounds," an amount that he considered dismaying at first glance.[77]

In Number 120, Sherman ordered the soldiers to stay out of the dwellings of citizens, but he provided language that sanctioned "more or less relentless" devastation. With a license to steal, confiscate and destroy within several dozen miles on either side of the routes being followed by the army, the foragers turned to their new assignments with vigor, stealing not only cattle, horses, hams and food, but all the silver and gold, jewelry and valuables they could find. They quickly learned that they would not be stopped or disciplined as long as they kept 10 days provisions for the army and three days of forage for the livestock. Receiving only praise for their escalating pillaging and with Sherman's tacit approval of the burning, the foragers, who became known as the bummers, could be tracked in their paths surrounding the regular army by the billowing smoke as they became increasingly more aggressive with their pillaging and stealing and destruction of everything in their wake.

General Wade Hampton
Courtesy of the South Caroliniana Library at the University of South Carolina, Columbia, S.C.

The lenient policy that covered the ever increasing destruction of everything in his path was an enormous part of the psychological warfare that Sherman waged as he marched his troops out of Atlanta on November 15. "Behind us lay Atlanta, smouldering and in ruins, the black smoke rising high in air, and hanging like a pall over the ruined city," he said.[78] It would become a common sight as the foragers surrounded the troops over miles of countryside in every direction in search of food, forage and livestock. Even before his full campaign had been approved by Grant, Sherman had planned his strategy. "I had no purpose to march direct for Richmond by way of Augusta and Charlotte, but always designed to reach the sea-coast first at

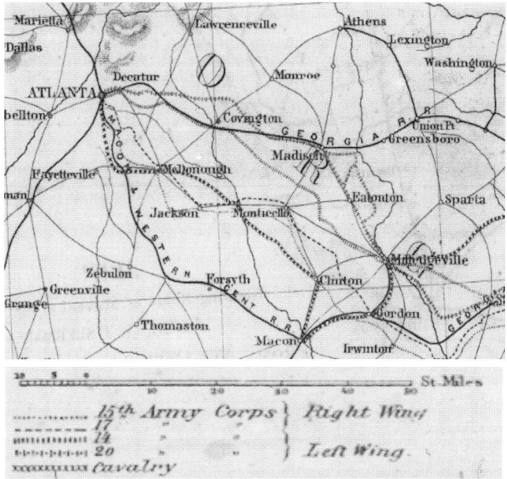

Sherman's march through Georgia ranged over a swath of dozens of miles.
Source: Library of Congress

Savannah or Port Royal, South Carolina, and even kept in mind the alternative of Pensacola.[79]

"I feel no doubt whatever as to our future plans," he said. "I have thought them over so long and well that they appear as clear as daylight. I left Augusta untouched on purpose, because the enemy will be in doubt as to my objective point, after we cross the Savannah River, whether it be Augusta or Charleston, and will naturally divide his forces." At the time he made his decision, Augusta had the largest powder factory remaining in the South.[80]

"I will then move either on Branchville or Columbia, by any curved line that gives us the best supplies, breaking up in our course as much railroad as possible; then, ignoring Charleston and Augusta both, I would occupy Columbia and Camden, pausing there long enough to observe the effect. I would then strike for the Charleston & Wilmington Railroad, somewhere between the Santee and Cape Fear Rivers.... Then I would favor an attack on Wilmington."[81] He was confident that he could break up the whole railway system of South and North Carolina and on the Roanoke, either at Raleigh or Weldon, by spring.[82]

The robberies and pillaging by Sherman's "bummers" who had fanned out for miles in every direction was so common that every town in their path reported hundreds of incidents. The confiscated hams, bacon, cornmeal, livestock, other supplies and forage were turned over to the commissary along the line of march.

However, the stolen treasure was another matter. The loot, consisting of gold, silver and other valuables, was supposed to be returned to camp and turned over to the commissary to be shared among the troops in a strictly regulated manner, just like the animals, food and other supplies, according to Myers, but apparently many of the valuables, especially small items like jewelry and diamonds, were hidden and never reported.[83]

Although Myers would later describe Sherman's complicity in the division of booty, Sherman never admitted or denied taking part in the distribution of loot. He did admit that he was aware of the violent plundering, which he made no effort to stop and dismissed as only "occasional incidents."

"No doubt, many acts of pillage, robbery and violence, were committed by these parties of foragers, usually called 'bummers;' for I have since heard of jewelry taken from women and the plunder of articles that never reached the commissary." But he insisted that these acts "were exceptional and incidental."[84]

In downplaying the pillaging and plundering, he even inadvertently admitted that jewelry and other valuables that were stolen and robbed were supposed to be turned over to the commissary, a central point in Myers' description of the method of distribution.[85]

In spite of Sherman's efforts to downplay the extent of the plundering, the pillaging and looting were far from "exceptional and incidental," as witnessed by the avalanche of diaries, letters, personal accounts and newspaper stories describing cruel and frightening efforts to find silver, gold and jewelry—which was frequently accompanied by threats, violence and brutality.

However, Sherman never wavered from the defense of his army, no matter how barbaric, or his total war on civilians—and even, according to Myers, his willingness to take his share of the loot that was divided in the camps. The foraging was so successful, Sherman crowed when he reached Savannah, that the horses and mules pulling the wagon trains "were pronounced by experts to be the finest in flesh and appearance ever seen with any army."[86]

Marching an average of 12 to 15 miles a day, the army had by November 20 marched 75 miles southeast of Atlanta to Eatonton Factory and the plantation of Confederate General Howell Cobb, who had been Secretary of the U.S. Treasury under President James Buchanan. Although Sherman's general orders provided leeway— and his demeanor gave encouragement—for pillaging and destruction, Sherman himself rarely gave the actual order. However, when he determined that the plantation in Eatonton belonged to a Confederate general, he personally ordered the men to confiscate everything "and to spare nothing."[87]

After Sherman's army had marched 100 miles to Milledgeville on November 23, Sherman gave general orders for the cavalry to make a side trip of about 85 miles toward Millen to rescue prisoners of war at a camp recently established to take the overflow from Andersonville. The right wing followed the Savannah Railroad, and the left wing moved on to Sandersville by Davisboro and Louisville.[88]

Although Sherman's troops had marched without opposition as far as Milledgeville, Sherman found that Wheeler was ahead of him between Milledgeville and Augusta and Hardee had been dispatched from Hood's army to oppose Sherman's progress. Beauregard was also in Georgia by then, but had brought no troops and was trying to raise militia from the countryside.[89]

The Federal army reached Milledgeville on November 23 where Sherman occupied the governor's mansion and destroyed public buildings, and armories and other government structures that could have been used by Confederates[90] along with 1,700 bales of cotton. "Private houses were respected everywhere, even those of noted Rebels, and I heard of no instance of pillage or insult to the inhabitants," Nichols said.[91] When Sherman's troops reached Sandcrsville on November 26, Sherman told some citizens that if the enemy attempted to carry out their threat to burn their food, corn and fodder in his route, "I would most undoubtedly execute to the letter the general orders of devastation made at the outset of the campaign." He would later say that with minor exceptions, the people did not destroy food, for "they saw clearly that it would be ruin to themselves."[92] However, in spite of civilian cooperation with Sherman's terms, the bummers continued to pillage and destroy at will as they rampaged through the countryside.

By time Sherman reached Millen on December 3, Confederate General Braxton Bragg had reached Augusta, Georgia, and General Wade Hampton had been ordered to South Carolina from Richmond to organize a cavalry force to resist Sherman's advance.[93]

Hampton and his cavalry had been the "ears and eyes" of the Army of Northern Virginia. It was their business to protect the railway communications from the enemy, to insure Richmond against all raiding parties, to capture wagon trains of the enemy, destroy their depots, report their movements and ascertain their plans of attack. Hampton's men were in a cavalry skirmish almost every day, and he had been at all the large battles—at Wilderness, Spottsylvania, Cold Harbor and others. He frequently dismounted his men and fought them as infantry, using the carbine, and "thus introduced a new method of cavalry fighting."[94]

Hardee was ahead of Sherman along with General Lafayette McLaws, but Sherman estimated the total troops of Hardee and McLaws as no more than 10,000 men. Sherman had expected to find Federal prisoners in recently established Camp Lawton in Millen, but the prisoners had been moved and the camp was deserted. Sherman personally ordered his soldiers to destroy the depot and most of Millen.[95]

By December 5, Sherman's troops were about 50 miles from Savannah, and the columns marched leisurely toward the city. Corn and forage were becoming scarcer, but rice fields along the Savannah and Ogeechee rivers were proving a good substitute.[96]

4 FORTY ACRES AND A MULE

I have no doubt the State of Georgia has lost, by our operations, fifteen thousand first-rate mules.

—*William T. Sherman*

By the time Sherman approached Savannah, his troops were being followed by "thousands"[97] of freedmen even though some of his troops were taking measures to discourage the emancipated slaves from following in their path.

More than two thousand freed slaves were following U.S. General Jefferson C. Davis (no relationship to the Confederate president) on December 9 when he camped near Ebenezer Creek, a 165-foot-wide creek located 20 miles north of Savannah. General Joseph Wheeler trained a battery of 12-pound guns on their camp in the darkness and began shelling the position while the soldiers were sleeping. The Federals fled over a narrow pontoon bridge over the creek, leaving horses, arms, knapsacks and the entire camp equipage behind."[98]

The soldiers crowded the fugitive slaves off the bridge to save themselves, and then when Davis ordered the bridge drawn up before the remaining slaves could cross, frightened men, women, and children plunged into the deep water to follow. Some drowned in the attempt, and Wheeler rounded up the remaining slaves—"about two thousand in number"—and sent them back to their owners, under guard.[99]

After the deaths of the slaves, Davis was criticized in the Northern press, but Sherman defended his officer, saying that Davis had done what was militarily necessary.[100]

"On the occasion referred to, the bridge was taken up from Ebenezer Creek while some of the camp-followers remained asleep on the farther side," Sherman said, "and these were picked up by Wheeler's cavalry. Some of them, in their fright, were drowned in trying to swim over, and others may have been cruelly killed by Wheeler's men, but this was a mere supposition."[101]

Sherman and Wheeler both described the incident in a somewhat similar way except for the murder charge, which was one of Sherman's many "mystification" charges. The accusation caught the attention of the Lincoln administration, and Secretary of War Stanton looked with interest at Sherman's charges about the pontoon bridge and Confederates killing runaway slaves instead of sending them back to their masters, as Wheeler did.[102]

All of Sherman's other efforts to blame Confederates worked perfectly during his campaign except for this one, which would have worked had he not accused Wheeler of "possibly killing" the slaves, but Sherman's accusation backfired when it reached Washington, D.C.

Lincoln's Secretary of War Stanton disliked Sherman and saw a coveted chance for political traction in the official report that contained the Wheeler murder charge. Stanton was anti-Lincoln, and the time was perfect. The "rebellion" had been virtually suppressed, and the new politics were at hand; so, Stanton helped escalate the Ebenezer incident into accusations about Sherman's harsh treatment and even "hatred" of the slaves who followed in his wake.

General Jefferson Davis (no relation to the Confederate President) confers with one of his officers in his headquarters tent. The writing desk at his right elbow is typical of the field cabinets that were used by officers during the Civil War. Source: Library of Congress

Cannons still stand guard at Fort McAllister on the Ogeechee River and parts of the Atlantic Ocean south of Savannah, Georgia. Live oaks draped with Spanish moss stand sentinel at the sand and mud earth works, which were attacked seven times before falling to Sherman's forces in 1864. The historic park contains a museum of Civil War artifacts. Source: Library of Congress

It would not be the only time during Sherman's march to North Carolina that slaves drowned while trying to follow the troops, but the Ebenezer Creek incident was the only one that drew the attention of the Lincoln administration. It also would not be Stanton's last effort to discredit Sherman.

In contrast to the plans Sherman had hatched in Atlanta, the orders that he received from Grant on December 6 were for him to march to Savannah and to move his command to Virginia by sea.[103] Sherman was not happy with those orders and was still thinking about his own ambitious plans when on December 10 he sent General

William B. Hazen with 4,000 Federals to overwhelm a Confederate force of about 120 men at earthen Fort McAllister, south of Savannah. The victory on December 13 provided the Union Army with control of the Ogeechee River, an avenue to the ocean, and opened the back door to the port city.

In a letter on December 16, Sherman told Grant that he would be bringing 50,000 or 60,000 men to City Point, "and incidentally to

General William B. Hazen
Source: Library of Congress

capture Savannah, if time will allow."[104] But arriving in City Point by sea was not what Sherman had planned in Atlanta and not what he wanted to do, so he proposed to Grant his plan to march through the Carolinas instead of embarking by sea. He described how well the troops had performed in Georgia and explained with great enthusiasm that his troops had reached Savannah "in splendid flesh and condition." He said that 65,000 men and 35,000 animals had been well fed for about 40 days.[105] He described the "liberal and judicious foraging" that had allowed his army to reach the seacoast with abundant forage and provisions, lacking nothing on arrival except bread.

"Of this, we started from Atlanta, with from eight to twenty days' supply per corps and some of the troops only had one day's issue of bread during the trip of thirty days; yet they did not want, for sweet-potatoes were very abundant, as well as corn-meal, and our soldiers took to them naturally," he wrote.[106] Sherman's troops had started with about 5,000 head of cattle, and arrived with more than 10,000, "of course, consuming mostly turkeys, chickens, sheep, hogs, and the cattle of the country."[107]

Sherman had left Atlanta with about 2,500 wagons, many of which were drawn by mules that had not recovered from the Chattanooga starvation, so the mules in poor condition had been shot and replaced with healthy animals. "I have no doubt the State of

Georgia has lost, by our operations, fifteen thousand first-rate mules," he said. Sherman did not estimate the number of horses, but noted the practice was "for each brigade to send out daily a foraging party of about 50 men on foot who invariably returned mounted, with several wagons loaded with poultry, potatoes, etc., and as the army is composed of about 40 brigades, you can estimate approximately the number of horses collected."[108] According to Sherman's numbers, at least 2,000 foragers on foot were pillaging and plundering the

The incident at Ebenezer Creek 20 miles north of Savannah became a national problem for Sherman before his troops crossed the Savannah River into South Carolina at Sisters Ferry and the lower Beaufort district to head for Pocotaligo.
Source: Library of Congress

countryside and bringing back livestock, poultry, vegetables, mules and as many as 2,000 horses a day. "Great numbers of these (horses) wcrc shot by my order, because of the disorganizing effect on our infantry of having too many idlers mounted," Sherman said. In 30 days, according to Sherman's numbers, the foragers would have brought back up to 60,000 horses, but many would have been shot.[109]

Faced with a surplus of mules and horses that the Federals captured to "deprive our enemy of them," Sherman arranged to have thousands of mules and horses sent to Port Royal, which had been held by the Federals since late 1861, or to be collected behind Fort McAllister or for the Quartermaster's Department.[110]

Before hearing from Grant, Sherman sent a letter to Hardee demanding the surrender of Savannah and

General William J. Hardee
Source: Library of Congress

giving him "a reasonable time to answer" before he would open with heavy ordnance. "I am prepared to grant liberal terms to the inhabitants and garrison," Sherman wrote, "but should I be forced to resort to assault, or the slower and surer process of starvation, I shall then feel justified in resorting to the harshest measures, and shall make little effort to restrain my army—burning to avenge the national wrong which they attach to Savannah and other large cities which have been so prominent in dragging our country into civil war."[111]

When Hardee refused to surrender the city, Sherman considered his options. "The ground was difficult, and, as all former assaults had proved so bloody, I concluded to make one more effort to completely surround Savannah on all sides, so as further to excite

Hardee's fears, and, in case of success, to capture the whole of his army."[112]

Urged by Beauregard to pull out, Hardee decided on December 20 to evacuate Savannah and head north to defend Charleston. The Confederate troops, which Sherman estimated at about 6,000 infantry and "a mongrel mass" of 8,000 or 10,000 militia, slipped quietly out of the city on December 21, and Sherman rode triumphantly into Savannah on December 22 to settle into his headquarters in what is now known as the Green-Meldrim House at 14 West Macon Street on Madison Square.[113]

Knowing that a vessel leaving Savannah the next day would reach Fortress Monroe by Christmas, U.S. Treasury Agent A.G. Browne of Salem, Massachusetts,[114] suggested to Sherman that he might want to send a note on the ship to President Lincoln giving him Savannah—a "welcome Christmas gift to the President, Mr. Lincoln, who peculiarly enjoyed such pleasantry."[115] Sherman liked the idea

The Green-Meldrim house where Sherman made his headquarters in Savannah looks almost the same today. Source: Library of Congress

well enough to write a note on a slip of paper to be left at the telegraph office at Fortress Monroe for transmission: "Savannah, Georgia, December 22. To His Excellency President Lincoln, Washington, D.C.: I beg to present you, as a Christmas-gift the city of Savannah with one hundred and fifty heavy guns and plenty of ammunition, also about twenty five thousand bales of cotton."[116]

The message reached Lincoln on Christmas Eve and was distributed to the newspapers. While President Lincoln was opening the message containing his Savannah present, Sherman was proposing his Carolinas Campaign in a letter to Grant in an effort to get the general to issue new orders that would comply with Sherman's already hatched plans for the Carolinas.

Sherman's letter was calm and persuasive, and he did not mention vengeance and revenge as reasons to go inland through South Carolina. However, he was boldly frank in his letter to Halleck, saying, "The truth is, the whole army is burning with an insatiable desire to wreak vengeance upon South Carolina. I almost tremble at her fate, but feel that she deserves all that seems in store for her."[117] He frankly said, "I look upon Columbia as quite as bad as Charleston, and I doubt if we shall spare the public buildings there as we did at Milledgeville."[118]

He set the stage for increased destruction when he openly acknowledged that he would make no effort to restrain his men in South Carolina, and he had a long "blame" list. "Somehow, our men had got the idea that South Carolina was the cause of all our troubles; her people were the first to fire on Fort Sumter, had been in a great hurry to precipitate the country into civil war; and therefore on them should fall the scourge of war in its worst form. Taunting messages had also come to us, when in Georgia, to the effect that, when we should reach South Carolina, we would find a people less passive, who would fight us to the bitter end, daring us to come over, etc.; so that I saw and felt that we would not be able longer to restrain our men as we had done in Georgia."[119]

Howard said that there was a "sort of vengeance animating the army as it came into South Carolina" but he said he did not know whether the officers were in unison with the men.[120] Howard would later testify that much more property was destroyed in South

Carolina on the line of march than was destroyed in Georgia and North Carolina.[121]

Grant quickly approved Sherman's plan to march through the Carolinas and deployed a division to garrison Savannah so that Sherman would not have to leave any of his men in the city.[122] Grant told Sherman to hold Savannah but to establish an entrenched camp on the railroad between Savannah and Charleston, leaving Savannah as "the great depot of supply for the federal troops,"[123]

Grant wanted Sherman to march toward Branchville, which would give the Federals a position in the South from which to threaten the interior without marching over long, narrow causeways. Branchville was important because it was the point where the Charleston Railroad branched west to Hamburg and Augusta and north to Columbia, Greenville, Chester and Charlotte.

Grant suggested such a camp at Pocotaligo or Coosawatchie. He told Sherman to begin without delay, breaking up the railroads in South and North Carolina and joining the armies operating against Richmond as soon as possible. Grant said he would not make any

General George Meade dispenses passes to civilians in Savannah who want to leave after Sherman's troops occupied the city. Source: Library of Congress

suggestions about the routes Sherman should take.[124] That was just what Sherman wanted to hear because he had planned his route through the Carolinas while he was in Atlanta. Grant's ultimate goal in the new plan was for Sherman to cross the Roanoke in North Carolina.

From there it "is but a few days' march, and supplies could be collected south of the river to bring you through. I shall establish communication with you there, by steamboat and gunboat," Grant said. "I shall hope to hear from you soon, and to hear your plan, and about the time of starting."[125]

General Henry Halleck
Source: Library of Congress

Sherman wanted to enter South Carolina as quickly as possible, but before leaving Savannah, he set liberal occupation plans for the more than 20,000 people who were there when he arrived.

Since Sherman regarded the war as rapidly drawing to a close, he said it was becoming a political question as to what was to be done with the people of the South, both white and black, when the war was actually over. "I concluded to give them the option to remain or to join their friends in Charleston or Augusta, and so announced in general orders."[126]

Sherman's orders for Savannah very specifically included protection of private property with carefully itemized instructions that Sherman not only expected but knew would be followed to the letter. "Families should be disturbed as little as possible in their residences, and tradesmen allowed the free use of their shops, tools, etc.; churches, schools, and all places of amusement and recreation, should be encouraged, and streets and roads made perfectly safe to persons in their pursuits."[127] About 200 people, mostly families of men in the Confederate army, chose to follow the fortunes of their husbands and fathers and were sent in a steamboat under a flag of truce to Charleston harbor.

Sherman also provided the mayor with a large warehouse of rice, which when traded for flour, hams, sugar and coffee to be delivered free to the residents, would relieve "the most pressing wants until the revival of trade and business enabled the people to provide for themselves."[128] He even provided for the publication of two newspapers in Savannah with Federal editors who would be held to strictest accountability, as he did later for Charleston when it was occupied on February 18.[129] Nothing was destroyed in Savannah, which was converted into a Federal supply depot.

Welcome news came to Sherman about his comrades in Tennessee, who had decoyed Hood to Nashville and defeated his army, capturing all his artillery and great numbers of prisoners, and were still pursuing the remainder of Hood's army in Alabama.[130]

Ruminating about his own simultaneous success, Sherman said, "I considered this march as a means to an end, and not as an essential act of war. Still, then, as now, the march to the sea was generally

The editors of the two Savannah newspapers fled just before Sherman's troops occupied the city. Sherman appointed two Federal editors to begin publishing again. The first edition after Sherman's occupation was The Loyal Georgian, which was published for two weeks before the title changed to the original local title of the Savannah Republican. Courtesy of the Irvin Department of Rare Books and Special Collections in the Ernest F. Hollings Special Collections Library at the University of South Carolina, Columbia, S.C.

regarded as something extraordinary, something anomalous, something out of the usual order of events; whereas, in fact, I simply moved from Atlanta to Savannah, as one step in the direction of Richmond, a movement that had to be met and defeated, or the war was necessarily at an end."[131]

In assessing the relative importance of the march to the sea compared to his planned march from Savannah through the Carolinas, Sherman said he would rate the march to the sea as a mere "one," but the march to the north at "ten, or the maximum."[132]

As Sherman arrived in Savannah, "tens of thousands of freedmen" had followed his troops and were camped nearby, but "because I had not loaded down my army by other hundreds of thousands of poor negroes, I was construed by others as hostile to the black race,"[133] Sherman said.

Soon after Christmas, he received a troubling letter on December 30 from Halleck, who said Sherman was being criticized in Washington for his treatment of the slaves.

General Jefferson Davis (no relation to the Confederate president)
Source: Library of Congress

"They say that you have manifested an almost criminal dislike to the negro, and that you are not willing to carry out the wishes of the Government in regard to him, but repulse him with contempt! They say you might have brought with you to Savannah more than fifty thousand, thus stripping Georgia of that number of laborers, and opening a road by which as many more could have escaped from their masters; but that, instead of this, you drove them from your ranks, prevented their following you by cutting the bridges in your rear, and thus caused the massacre of large numbers by Wheeler's cavalry."[134] In spite of the cutting criticism, Halleck said he was standing with Sherman during the controversy.

"To those who know you as I do," Halleck wrote Sherman, "such accusation will pass as the idle winds, for we presume that you discouraged the negroes from following you because you had not the means of supporting them, and feared they might seriously embarrass your march. But there are others, and among them some in high authority, who think or pretend to think otherwise, and they are decidedly disposed to make a point against you."[135]

Halleck said he was not trying to induce Sherman to "conciliate this class of men by doing anything which you do not deem right and proper, and for the interest of the Government and the country; but simply to call your attention to certain things which are viewed here somewhat differently than from your stand point."[136]

Some in Washington, Halleck said, were thinking that, in view of the scarcity of labor in the South and the probability that "a part, at least, of the able-bodied slaves would be called into the Confederate military service, that it would be of the greatest importance to open outlets by which these slaves can escape into our lines.... And they say that the route you have passed over should be made the route of escape, and Savannah the great place of refuge. These, I know, are the views of some of the leading men in the Administration, and they now express dissatisfaction that you did not carry them out in your great raid."[137]

Continuing with his line of reasoning, Halleck said, "Now that you are in possession of Savannah, and there can be no further fears about supplies, would it not be possible for you to reopen these avenues of escape for the negroes, without interfering with your military operations? Could not such escaped slaves find at least a partial supply of food in the rice fields about Savannah, and cotton plantations on the coast?"[138]

Halleck said that he was merely throwing out suggestions, but the inference in his last sentence was clear. "I know that such a course would be approved by the Government, and I believe that a manifestation on your part of a desire to bring the slaves within our lines will do much to silence your opponents." Halleck said he was sure Sherman would appreciate his motives in writing this private letter.[139] Sherman was outraged that his treatment of slaves was being questioned. He knew slavery was at an end, but he wanted to leave the fate of blacks up to themselves. Some politicians in Washington, primarily the Secretary of War, believed that Sherman thought blacks were inferior to the white man, "whether it was biology or history that made him so," and that he had evaded War Department attempts to make him enlist blacks as soldiers.[140]

Almost as soon as Sherman had finished reading the letter, Stanton arrived in Savannah to investigate the Ebenezer Creek incident and to question Sherman about his treatment of freed slaves and lack of their incorporation into the Federal Army. Stanton had read the accounts in the newspaper about the death of slaves at Ebenezer Creek, but he dropped that issue after hearing General Jeff Davis' explanation about Wheeler's attack on the camp and their quick exodus across the creek.

However, Stanton was not satisfied with Sherman's answer about his failure to incorporate slaves into his army. Although Sherman had reported that every regiment was followed by "at least fifty negroes and foot-sore soldiers, riding on horses and mules,"[141] he told Stanton that "... in our army we had no negro soldiers, and, as a rule, we preferred white soldiers, but ... we employed a large force of them as servants, teamsters, and pioneers, who had rendered admirable service."[142]

To pacify Stanton, Sherman arranged a meeting between Stanton and twenty leaders from the black community, mostly Baptist and Methodist preachers. When Stanton asked the leaders to "state in what manner you would rather live—whether scattered among the whites, or in colonies by yourselves," all the delegates except one agreed that they would prefer to live by themselves "for there is a prejudice against us in the South that will take years to get over."[143]

When Stanton asked how to increase the number of young black men in Sherman's army, their spokesman, Garrison Frazier, said, "I think, sir, that all compulsory operations should be put a stop to. The ministers would talk to them, and the young men would enlist. It is my opinion that it would be far better for the State agents to stay at home, and the enlistments be made for the United States under the direction of General Sherman."[144]

Stanton asked Sherman to leave the room so he could ask the black delegation how they felt about Sherman. They characterized him as a "friend and gentleman,"[145] but Sherman considered it odd that he should be sent out of the room for Stanton to ask questions about his integrity. "It certainly was a strange fact that the great War Secretary should have catechized negroes concerning the character of a general who had commanded a hundred thousand men in battle, had captured cities, conducted sixty-five thousand men successfully across four hundred miles of hostile territory, and had just brought tens of thousands of freedmen to a place of security; but because I had not loaded down my army by other hundreds of thousands of poor negroes, I was construed by others as hostile to the black race."[146]

Before Stanton left Savannah, Sherman drafted Special Field Orders No. 15, a temporary provision approved by Stanton for land grants for freedmen and their families during the rest of the war, or until Congress should take action. Sherman made it very clear that the military authorities "did not undertake to give a fee-simple title; and all that was designed by these special field orders was to make temporary provisions for the freedmen and their families during the rest of the war, or until Congress should take action in the premises." Assistant Adjutant General L.M. Dayton issued Sherman's orders on January 16 in Savannah that said that "the islands from Charleston south, the abandoned rice-fields along the rivers for thirty miles back from the sea and the country bordering the St. John's River, Florida, are reserved and set apart for the settlement of the negroes now made free by the acts of war and the proclamation of the President of the United States."[147]

The order also said that at Beaufort, Hilton Head, Savannah, Fernandina, St. Augustine and Jacksonville, "the blacks may remain in their chosen or accustomed vocation; but on the islands, and in the settlements hereafter to be established, no white person whatever, unless military officers and soldiers detailed for duty, will be permitted to reside; and the sole and exclusive management of affairs will be left to the freed people themselves subject only to the United States military authority, and the acts of Congress."[148] General R. Saxton was appointed Inspector of Settlements and Plantations.

The plan provided for not more than 40 acres of land for each family head, subject to the approval of the President of the United

States. Sherman considered that the land titles would be treated "as possessory...until such time as they can protect themselves or until Congress shall regulate their title."[149]

The establishment of a Freedmen's Bureau in March 1865 did little to resolve the conflict between returning property owners and freedmen with Sherman "titles." After Lincoln's assassination, property owners took the loyalty oath and wanted to return to their land; so President Andrew Johnson vetoed the Sherman Special Order as a violation of the constitutional rights of the property owners. Finally, Congress extended the right to Sherman "title holders" the privilege of buying at $1.50 an acre a 20-acre plot to be provided from several thousand acres in the Port Royal area.[150]

President Johnson vetoed the measure, but the veto was overridden, and the way was cleared for previous landowners to return to their land but for freed slaves to buy property. By July 1866, 1,398 former slaves had bought land, but most of the plots were for less than 20 acres. Most were for 10 acres, and some were for as few as two acres.[151]

Even before Sherman reached Savannah, hundreds of emancipated slaves had been living and working at federally held Port Royal, and after Sherman issued his military order, thousands more left for the sea islands and plantations along the coast. However, the order that provided for Sherman "titles" from Charleston to Jacksonville, Florida, did not end Sherman's problems with freedmen. Instead of going to Port Royal or any of the other lands and sea islands set aside by Sherman, hundreds of freed slaves continued to follow his troops as they headed north.

By the time Sherman reached Fairfield County in South Carolina, Alice Buchanan Walker who witnessed Sherman's march through Fairfield County, said that "more than 1,200 slaves were following the Yankee army from this locality under the belief that they were to be given forty acres of land, a mule, and a milch cow," she said. "In crossing over to the Lancaster County side of Catawba River on flat boats and rafts, many of these Negroes were drowned. Many found their way back, naked and half dead from cold and hunger."[152]

5 'A CLOUD OF SMOKE BY DAY, A PILLAR OF FIRE BY NIGHT'

An intensely bitter feeling was manifested by our troops from the moment they set foot on South Carolina soil. This remark would often be heard: 'Here is where treason began, and by God, here is where it shall end."

—*Colonel Charles Stone*

Having served as a First Lieutenant in the Third Artillery at Fort Moultrie from 1842 to 1846, Sherman was intimately familiar with South Carolina, so he had decided to march inland and "leave the rebel garrisons on the coast, instead of dislodging them and piling them up in my front as we progressed."[153] Sherman's goal was to secure a foothold in South Carolina at Pocotaligo and Hardeeville in modern-day Jasper County as the points of rendezvous for the two wings.[154]

"I will start with my Atlanta army (sixty thousand) supplied as before, depending on the country for all food in excess of thirty days," he wrote. "I will have less cattle on the hoof, but I hear of hogs, cows

Pocotaligo was an important stop on the Charleston and Savannah Railroad and an early foothold for Sherman in South Carolina. Source: Library of Congress

47

and calves, in Barnwell, and the Columbia districts. Even here we have found some forage. Of course, the enemy will carry off and destroy some forage, but I will burn the houses where the people burn their forage, and they will get tired of it."[155]

Orders were distributed to his generals on January 2, and the 17th Corps headed for Pocotaligo. Heavy winter rains delayed their progress, and the Savannah River was so swollen that it swept away their pontoon-bridge and nearly drowned a division of the 15th Corps.

The first general orders for the two wings to leave Savannah did not come until January 19:

> Right wing to move men and artillery by transports to head of Broad River and Beaufort; reestablish Port Royal Ferry, and mass the wing at or in the neighborhood of Pocotaligo.

> Left wing and cavalry to work slowly across the causeway toward Hardeeville, to open a road by which wagons can reach their corps about Broad River; also, by a rapid movement of the left to secure Sister's Ferry (about 40 miles north on the Savannah River), and Augusta road out to Robertville.

> In the meantime, all guns, shot, shell, cotton, etc., to be moved to a safe place, easy to guard, and provisions and wagons got ready for another swath, aiming to have our army in hand about the head of Broad River, say Pocotaligo, Robertville, and Coosawhatchie, by the 15th January.

> The whole army to move with loaded wagons by the roads leading in the direction of Columbia, which afford the best chance of forage and provisions. Howard to be at Pocotaligo by the 15th January, and Slocum to be at Robertville, and Kilpatrick at or near Coosawhatchie about the same date. General (Robert S.) Foster's troops to occupy Savannah, and gunboats to protect the rivers as soon as Howard gets Pocotaligo."[156]

Sherman's chosen objective was north through Columbia to Goldsboro, North Carolina,[157] but in one of his many acts of disinformation designed to confuse the Confederates as to his real line of march in South Carolina, Sherman dispatched troops toward Charleston and Augusta.[158]

Although military feints were normal acts of war, Sherman added to the deception by deliberately giving out more false information, "especially among the rebels, that we were going to Charleston or Augusta, but I had long before made up my mind to waste no time on either, further than to play off on their fears, thus to retain for their protection a force of the enemy which would otherwise concentrate in our front, and make the passage of some of the great rivers that crossed our route more difficult and bloody."[159]

William Gilmore Simms was the leading literary figure in the South before the Civil War. Even though his plantation was located in Bamberg, he was living and working in Columbia as co-editor of The Daily South Carolinian. Source: Library of Congress

Sherman's feints and misleading information were working perfectly. William Gilmore Simms, nationally known author and co-editor of the *Daily South Carolinian* in Columbia, would later write: "In truth, there was no small portion of the inhabitants (of Columbia) who denied or doubted, almost to the last moment, that Sherman contemplated any serious demonstration upon the city. They assumed—and this idea was tacitly encouraged, if not believed, by the authorities, military and civil—that the movement on Columbia was but a feint, and that the bulk of his army was preparing for a descent upon Charleston. This also seemed to be the opinion in Charleston itself."[160]

Sherman estimated the distance from Savannah to Goldsboro via Columbia as being 425 miles, and his army would be crossing five large navigable rivers, including the Edisto, Broad, Catawba, and the Pee Dee in South Carolina and Cape Fear, North Carolina. "The country was in a state of nature," Sherman said, "with innumerable swamps, with simply mud roads, nearly every mile of which had to be corduroyed," which meant logs or poles had to be placed side by side across swampy or unstable ground to provide a road.[161]

The actual strength of the army was 60,079 men and 68 guns with about 2,500 wagons, with six mules to each wagon; about 600 ambulances with two horses each, "and enough ammunition for a great battle, forage for seven days, provisions for 20 days and fresh meat on beeves driven on the hoof and such cattle, hogs and poultry as we expected to gather along our line of march."[162]

Sherman's troops built dozens of miles of corduroy roads through much of South Carolina. Because of constant rain and swamps and creeks, soldiers had to lay logs or poles across unstable ground for the troops to pass. Source: Library of Congress

Slocum ferried the rest of the left wing along with Kilpatrick's cavalry across the Savannah at Sister's Ferry, about forty miles north of Savannah. The left wing, under the command of Slocum, crossed two divisions of the 20th Corps over the Savannah River above the city and occupied Hardeeville with one division and Purysburg with another.[163] Sherman's soldiers attacked Hardeeville with such ferocity that the town completely disappeared, and "two or three piles of blackened bricks and an acre or so of dying embers marked the site of an old revolutionary town (of Purysburg) and this before the column had fairly got its hand in."[164] When the troops burned Bluffton, only the Episcopal Church survived because it was protected by a grove of oak trees, but the church was suspended after the townsfolk fled.[165]

Historian Alan Nevins described the change that came over Sherman's army when it crossed the Savannah and sensed it was

General Henry Slocum, commander of Sherman's left wing.
Source: Library of Congress

heading northward toward home. "'Every soldier felt he was in the heart of the enemy's country and it was his duty to do all the damage possible to the enemy,'" he quotes a veteran of the march. Houses were set on fire "'so near the road...it became so hot our ammunition trains were obliged to go out in the fields to pass. If we halted to rest in a little town, it would be but a short time before houses all about seemed to be in flames." The scene was repeated "all across the state.'" Not only did no one have orders "to do this work of destruction, but on the contrary it was strictly forbidden.'" Yet it happened. An Illinois major recalled, "The army burnt everything that it came near in South Carolina, not under orders but in spite of orders."[166]

Groups of Sherman's foragers styled themselves as "Wheeler's cavalry" who robbed and pillaged until the people denounced "Wheeler's cavalry" as worse than Sherman. An officer in the cavalry of U.S. General James H. Wilson confessed after the war that "the invading army had hundreds of their men distributed through the country, representing themselves as 'Wheeler's cavalry,' sent out on their work of theft and insult."[167]

General John Porter Hatch's division had reached Coosawatchie or Tullafinny, where the Charleston & Savannah Railroad crosses the Savannah River. Howard had collected the right wing on Beaufort Island by January 10 and had begun the 25-mile inland march to Pocotaligo. The right wing of the Federals crossed the island mainland on Saturday, January 14, by a pontoon bridge.[168]

While his troops were struggling through swollen rivers and streams to reach Pocotaligo and Robertville, Sherman embarked on a steamer from Savannah on January 21 with his headquarters staff en route to Beaufort by way of Hilton Head. Because of the rain and bad weather, he did not reach Beaufort until January 23. When the Federals reached Pocotaligo, they found that the fort had been abandoned. They had lost two officers and eight men in skirmishes,[169] but by then,

General Lafayette McLaws
Source: Library of Congress

most of General Francis Preston Blair's troops were on the railroad near Pocotaligo, near the head of the Broad River, where supplies were carried from Hilton Head by steamboats.

Sherman had determined that the two main wings would not be deployed out of Pocotaligo toward Columbia until February 1, so he had decided to go in person to Pocotaligo and act as though he was bound for Charleston. Sherman left Beaufort with part of his staff on January 24, crossing the channel between it and the mainland on a pontoon bridge and heading toward a plantation occupied by Blair, not far from Pocotaligo.

Remembering with fondness the years he spent in the Low Country while stationed at Fort Moultrie, Sherman said he had many

As Federals moved through the old Beaufort District in January, they burned the Old Sheldon Church, formerly known as the Prince William Parish Church. The Old Sheldon Ruins are still visible. Source: Library of Congress

friends in Charleston to whom he would gladly have extended protection and mercy, "but they were beyond my personal reach, and I would not restrain the army lest its vigor and energy should be impaired; and I had every reason to expect bold and strong resistance at the many broad and deep rivers that lay across our path."[170]

General Robert E. Lee.
Source: Library of Congress

The Federals fought their way through the old Beaufort District against Generals Wheeler, General Lafayette McLaws and Colonel Charles Colcock Jones, Jr., and burned their way through Lawtonville, Hickory Hill, Whippy Swamp and Broxton's Bridge.[171] As Federals moved through the old Beaufort District, they burned the Old Sheldon Church, formerly known as the Prince William Parish Church.[172] The church had been burned by the British in 1780 and rebuilt in 1830. The ruins are still visible today.[173]

As they moved toward the Combahee River, the Mission Chapel in the same parish was taken down by Sherman's troops to build a bridge over the river. The Ashepoo Church in St. Bartholomew's Parish was left standing, but weatherboarding and flooring was also used by the Federals to build a bridge over the river. Every planter's house was burned for miles around, and the population generally dispersed.[174]

Colonel Charles Stone, who would accept the Columbia surrender letter on February 17, wrote:

"An intensely bitter feeling was manifested by our troops from the moment they set foot on South Carolina soil. In no other seceded state was there any particular ill feeling shown toward the inhabitants. But from one end of the first-named state to the other it might truly be said that our march was marked by 'a cloud of smoke by day and a pillar of fire by night.' My recollection is that, outside of the towns, not a house was left standing unless occupied by negroes, and from the dense clouds of smoke, a few miles each to our right and left—plainly defining the march of the columns advancing in parallel lines—it seemed that the same destruction was following in the wake of these columns. One instance—I could give 20—will illustrate and show the animus of the troops."[175]

Mary Boykin Chesnut was the author of "A Diary from Dixie," considered one of the most important and influential Civil War books by a Confederate author.
Courtesy of the South Caroliniana Library at the University of South Carolina, Columbia, S.C.

Stone described an evening when he halted the rear guard to camp within three miles of a fine mansion. Fearing that the mansion would meet the fate of every other house along the route, he guarded the house himself until the troops arrived within their picket lines.

About midnight, he saw a fire in the direction of the house and found the next morning that even though his men had marched 27 miles the day before, some of them had marched six more miles in the middle of the night to burn that house. "This remark would often be heard: 'Here is where treason began, and by God! here is where it shall end,'" Stone said.[176]

Knowing that his plantation home in Bamberg was in the line of march and had already been destroyed once by Federal troops, Simms followed the news of their progress with dread.

"The march of the Federals into South Carolina was characterized by such scenes of license, plunder and general conflagration, as very soon showed that the 'threats of the Northern press, and of their soldiery, were not to be regarded as mere *brutum fulmen*,'"[177] (or futile threat).

While Sherman was establishing a foothold in South Carolina, the Confederate Senate passed a resolution on January 16 asking that Robert E. Lee should be appointed commander-in-chief of the armies of the Confederacy. Beauregard was appointed commander in South Carolina, Georgia and Florida, while General Joe Johnston regained command of the Army of Tennessee.

Thus, Beauregard was again in charge of the troops in South Carolina as he had been on April 14, 1861, when shots were first fired at Fort Sumter in Charleston. Beauregard was hoping to assemble about 33,500 men to oppose Sherman's 60,000-man army, but in actuality only about 25,000 Confederate forces were left in South Carolina when Sherman's troops entered the state.

Sherman considered Beauregard's "scattered and

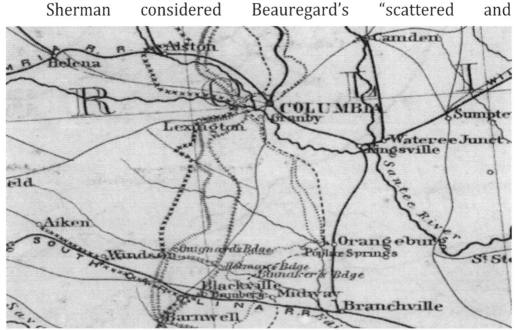

Sherman's troops assaulted Branchville, Midway, Barnwell, Bamberg, Blackville, Windsor, Aiken and Orangeburg and other small villages as they approached Columbia. The left wing continued on through Lexington to Alston to cross the Broad River toward Fairfield County while the right wing crossed the Broad River into Columbia.

Source: Library of Congress

inconsiderable forces" a mere nuisance, and predicted they would delay him only an hour.[178]

The Confederates did not know which direction Sherman would take through South Carolina. Charlestonians, who erroneously expected Sherman to come through Charleston, began shipping their goods—jewelry, liquor and valuables—to Columbia, including the bells of St. Michael's Episcopal Church that had been cast in England in 1764. Although many bells in the South had been recast for artillery, St. Michael's bells had survived, but were sent inland for safety. They were stored on the State House grounds in Columbia and cracked when Federals set fire to the shed in which they were stored during the burning of Columbia.[179]

Gen. James Chesnut, Jr., C.S.A.

General James Chesnut was Mary Boykin Chesnut's husband and one of Confederate President Jefferson Davis' aides. Chesnut ordered the firing at Fort Sumter. Courtesy of the South Carolinana Library at the University of South Carolina, Columbia, S.C.

As Sherman marched, refugees poured into Columbia from all over the state, swelling the population from 7,000 to almost 20,000. Sherman's advance guards skirmished with Confederates along the Salkehatchie River on January 25, but, exactly as Sherman had hoped, Beauregard ordered Hardee to defend Charleston and General D.H. Hill to defend Augusta, Georgia, where the largest powder factory in the Confederacy was located. Hardee established a defense along the Salkehatchie River, a tributary of the Combahee River, and prepared to retreat toward Charleston once Sherman's troops penetrated the entrenchments.[180]

That left Beauregard with a single cavalry brigade to protect the Confederate-held railroad junction at Branchville after Sherman crossed the South Fork of the Edisto River.[181]

Colonel Welles Jones Brigade cross at Shillings Bridge on the Edisto River on a raft before the pontoons are laid and are charging on the enemy's works. The men shown on the left are crossing on a floating footbridge. Source: Library of Congress

While Sherman was crossing the Edisto, Grant was receiving in his Virginia headquarters CSA vice president Alexander Stephens and CSA representatives who wanted to approach President Lincoln about a peace initiative. Lincoln agreed with all except one of the Confederate demands, including the continuation of slavery, but he insisted on the seceded states rejoining the Union. The peace talks failed when the Confederate commissioners rejected his demand.[182] The visit might have been unknown or not sanctioned by President Davis who was busy dispatching General James Connor with his small brigade from the trenches at Petersburg to his home in Charleston, as well as General James Chesnut, who had been a United States senator, to Columbia, where he and his wife, Mary Boykin Chesnut, had a rental home.

Davis also dispatched young General Matthew Butler's division of South Carolina cavalry, to his native state. Lee was seriously crippled, and Beauregard had no assistance. By February 1, Confederates had garrisons in Charleston and Aiken, and Hampton, chief of Lee's cavalry and the most beloved of all South Carolinians, had arrived from the Army of Virginia in his home state. He was near

Columbia with two small divisions of cavalry commanded by himself and Butler. Sherman said, "Hampton had been dispatched from the Army of Virginia to his native State of South Carolina, with a great flourish of trumpets, and extraordinary powers to raise men, money, and horses, with which 'to stay the progress of the invader,' and 'to punish us for our insolent attempt to invade the glorious State of South Carolina!'"[183]

In addition to disliking Hampton, Sherman had a low opinion of the forces left to defend South Carolina. Sherman said he "had a species of contempt" for the Confederates' small and scattered forces, "and the only serious question that occurred to me was, would General Lee sit down in Richmond (besieged by General Grant) and permit us, almost unopposed to pass through the States of South and North Carolina, cutting off and consuming the very supplies on which he depended to feed his army in Virginia, or would he make an effort to escape from General Grant, and endeavor to catch us inland somewhere between Columbia and Raleigh?"[184]

Sherman arranged for points of security along the coast at Bull's Bay and Georgetown, South Carolina, and along the mouth of Cape Fear River in North Carolina.

He estimated that Hardee, Wheeler and Hampton had 15,000 men in South Carolina, which, if combined with the remnants of Hood's army of 25,000 men, would mean 40,000 men, which Sherman thought "would constitute a formidable force, and might make the passage of such rivers as the Santee and Cape Fear a difficult undertaking."[185]

Therefore, Sherman planned to march swiftly before Hood's army could reach Columbia. Sherman's goal was to march 425 miles through South and North Carolina to Goldsboro, North Carolina, where two railroads met coming from Wilmington and Newbern, North Carolina.

"In general terms, my plan is to turn over to General (John Gray) Foster the city of Savannah, to sally forth with my army resupplied, cross the Savannah, feign on Charleston and Augusta, but strike between, breaking en route the Charleston & Augusta Railroad, also a large part of that from Branchville and Camden toward North Carolina, and then rapidly to move for some point of the railroad from

Charleston to Wilmington , between the Santee and Cape Fear Rivers; then communicating with the fleet in the neighborhood of Georgetown, I would turn upon Wilmington or Charleston, according to the importance of either," he said.[186]

"I rather prefer Wilmington, as a live place, over Charleston, which is dead and unimportant when its railroad communications are broken...If I should determine to take Charleston, I would turn across the country (which I have hunted over many a time) from Santee to Mount Pleasant, throwing one wing on the peninsula between the Ashley and Cooper. After accomplishing one or the other of the ends, I would make a bee-line for Raleigh or Weldon, when Lee would be forced to come out of Richmond, or acknowledge himself beaten."[187]

After the brief stay in Savannah, the foragers had been turned loose on the land to begin their pillaging and burning in South Carolina. "Here we are; and where our footsteps pass, fire, ashes and desolation follow in the path," Nichols said. "An armed force marching through the land is a fearful scourge."[188]

The lobby of Sherman's headquarters in the Green-Meldrim House in Savannah, Georgia. *Source: Library of Congress*

6 IS THE TARGET CHARLESTON OR AUGUSTA?

The roads were covered with butchered cattle, hogs, mules and the costliest furniture…. Horses were ridden into the houses. People were forced from their beds to permit the search after hidden treasures.

—William Gilmore Simms

"The actual invasion of South Carolina has begun, " Sherman's aide-de-camp Major George Nichols wrote on January 30, 1865. "The well known sign of columns of black smoke meets our gaze again. This time houses are burning, and South Carolina has commenced to pay an installment, long overdue, on her debt to justice and humanity. With the help of God, we will have principal and interest before we leave her borders. There is a terrible gladness in the realization of so many hopes and wishes. But here we are; and wherever our footsteps pass, fire, ashes and desolation follow…."[189]

The first troops were hardly in the state before McPhersonville was burned to the ground on January 31 followed by Hickory Hill on February 1 and plantations along the Ashley River just north of Charleston. The Federal right wing, which had feinted toward Charleston, was in Pocotaligo by February 1 with wagons filled with food, ammunition and forage, waiting for the left wing, which had been detained by the flood in the Savannah River.

The 17th U.S. Army Corps led by Major General Joseph A. Mower and Lieutenant General Giles A. Smith forged ahead with 5,000 men to face General Lafayette McLaws and his army of 1,200 Confederates, who were holding the crossings of the Salkehatchie River on February 2.

The Confederates had cut the bridges that spanned the deep channels of the swollen Salkehatchie River, but the Federal column, led by General Francis P. Blair, waded through the swamp in water up to their shoulders, crossed over to the pine land and attacked the Confederates on February 3 in what would become known as the Battle of Rivers Bridge.[190]

Approximately 6,200 soldiers clashed in this battle—5,000 Union soldiers and 1,200 Confederate. Two hundred and sixty-two men were killed—92 Union and 170 Confederate.

The skirmish with the outnumbered Confederate forces held up Sherman's march through South Carolina for two days.[191]

McLaws retreated toward Branchville on February 3 as Sherman's troops waded through the swamps along the Salkehatchie and headed north in the general direction of Columbia.[192]

Although the main house was rebuilt for the third time after the Civil War, this small brick building is all that is left of the original plantation of William Gilmore Simms. He did most of his writing here.
Source: Library of Congress

On February 4, Federals skirmished at Buford's Bridge before reaching a point 60 miles south of Columbia that was within five miles of Bamberg. The little town was the home of Woodlands, the 4,000-acre plantation owned by William Gilmore Simms. His home had been burned in 1863 by Federals and rebuilt, but it was burned again by Sherman's bummers as they hunted for supplies, forage and valuables after Sherman's main army destroyed Bamberg and moved on Orangeburg.[193] Howard would later shift blame from his troops by writing that "Mr. Simms' property was left in good condition."[194]

By early February 1865, Sherman's army had marched widely through lower South Carolina, destroying most small towns, including Brighton, Buford's Bridge[195] and Robertville.[196]

By February 5, Kilpatrick and his cavalry were on the railroad near Barnwell, the 15th Corps was approaching Bamberg and the 17th Corps was headed for Midway.[197] All would be destroyed.

Earthworks at Morris Ford on the Salkehatchie River in Barnwell County that were first built in the spring of 1780 by

Loyalists had been rebuilt by Confederate cavalry by Wheeler, who delayed the advancing Federal cavalry under Kilpatrick. On February 6, a sharp skirmish occurred at the works. Elements of Kilpatrick's force crossed downstream, outflanked the Confederate cavalry and forced it to withdraw, then advanced to Barnwell while Wheeler's cavalry withdrew toward Aiken. And Kilpatrick's cavalry burned most of Barnwell later that night.[198]

Federal cavalry under Kilpatrick advanced to Blackville on February 7. Colonel Thomas J. Jordan's brigade attacked a Confederate cavalry brigade, driving them through the town and three miles beyond in what would be known as the Battle of Blackville. Kilpatrick destroyed the railroad at Blackville and advanced west to Reynolds Station between Blackville and Williston.[199]

Sherman's had ordered Kilpatrick to attack Aiken to feint the army's objective as Augusta and destroy as much property as

Sherman chose General Judson Kilpatrick to lead the cavalry because he "displayed so much zeal and activity." Source: Library of Congress

possible, including the South Carolina Railroad as far as Augusta.[200]

On February 7, 1865, Sherman's troops passed through Gillisonville in old Beaufort District where they visited the Coosawhatchie Baptist Church (which became Gillisonville Baptist Church in 1885). One of Sherman's soldiers scratched "War of 1861 & 62 & 63 & 64 Feb 7th 1865 this is done by a Yankee Soldier" on the communion silver, but the soldiers spared the 1845 church building.[201]

Early on the morning of February 7, while Howard had been preparing to attack and destroy Midway, one of the foragers mounted on a white horse with a rope bridle and blanket for a saddle raced toward him to tell him that they had taken the railroad. "So while we, the generals were proceeding deliberately to prepare for a serious battle, a parcel of our foragers, in search of plunder, had got ahead and actually captured the South Carolina Railroad, a line of vital

Near the end of the war, General James Chesnut and his wife Mary Boykin Chesnut were living in this cottage at 1718 Plain (Hampton) Street in Columbia, where President Jefferson Davis delivered a speech from this porch in October 1864. The cottage is a Bed and Breakfast today. Photo by Pat McNeely

importance to the rebel Government," Sherman said.[202] By then, the Federals were in full control of the railroad. "Every tie burned and every rail twisted is an irretrievable damage to the Rebels," Nichols said.[203]

And thus, plundering and burning, the troops had made their way through Beaufort District into Barnwell District, Simms wrote. "The inhabitants everywhere (were) left homeless and without food. The horses and mules, all cattle and hogs, whenever fit for service or for food, were carried off, and the rest shot. Every implement of the workman or the farmer, tools, plows, hoes, gins, looms, wagons, vehicles, was made to feed the flames."[204]

Simms began itemizing the towns that Sherman's troops burned as they passed to include "all hamlets of most modest character, where no resistance was offered—where no fighting took place—where there was no provocation of liquor even, and when the only exercise of heroism was at the expense of women, infancy and feebleness."

Word of the mindless burning and pillaging as Sherman's troops foraged through the countryside reached Mary Boykin Chesnut, who was living in a cottage in Columbia instead of at her plantation home in Camden when word came on February 8 that Sherman's troops were approaching Orangeburg, which had a population of 3,000.[205] She packed quickly and left in "utter despair" on a 12-hour train ride to Charlotte, North Carolina, where she took a stagecoach to nearby Lincolnton, North Carolina.[206]

The Chesnut Cottage at 1718 Plain (Hampton) Street in Columbia was the temporary wartime home of General and Mrs. James Chesnut. They had entertained President Jefferson Davis and his staff there on October 5, 1864, and President Davis had addressed the citizens of Columbia from the front steps of this cottage.[207] Both the cottage in which the Chesnuts lived in Columbia and Mulberry, their plantation in Camden, were spared.

On February 10, Slocum's troops headed toward Orangeburg knowing now that their real goal was Columbia. However, as disinformation, Kilpatrick had been ordered to demonstrate strongly toward Aiken "to keep up the delusion" that the Federals were headed for Augusta when the real goal was to be Columbia.[208]

Kilpatrick's men advanced along the railroad, destroying it as they moved through Windsor on February 9. They camped the night of February 10 at Johnson's Turnout (Montmorenci) near Aiken, where they built long lines of barricades.[209]

"The general march was resumed on February 11, each corps crossing the South Edisto by separate bridges with orders to pause on the road leading from Orangeburg to Augusta, till it was certain that the 17th Corps had got possession of Orangeburg," Sherman wrote.[210]

Sherman was in a hurry because parts of Hood's army had reached Augusta, and Sherman wanted to reach Columbia before the arrival of fresh Confederate troops. With Sherman's troops divided into two wide-ranging main wings with feints toward Charleston and Augusta, skirmishes would occur as far west in South Carolina as Aiken and as far east as James Island near Charleston.

Pauline DeCaradeuc Heyward, who lived on a plantation near Aiken, described the Federal attack on her family's home on February 10. She said they asked for liquor, gold and silver and began stealing and destroying furniture and other finery in the house. "With axes

Federal soldiers pillage and rob a Confederate bedroom. *Source: Library of Congress*

they broke open every door, drawer, trunk that was locked, smashed a large French mirror, broke pieces of furniture and flung every piece of clothing, that they didn't carry off, all over the floors.... they carried off every piece of silver, every knife, jewel & particle of possession" on the plantation.[211]

While Kilpatrick was focused on Aiken, the defenders of Charleston fought Union troops from the sea and inland on February 10 on James Island and Johnson's Station. Reaching Aiken, Kilpatrick's troops skirmished with Wheeler's troops for three hours on February 11 before the Federals fell back to their infantry support near Montmorenci, where they were stationed.[212] It would be the only Confederate victory in South Carolina during Sherman's march through the state. Most importantly, Sherman's army cut the Augusta-Georgia railroad on February 11, which divided the Confederates assembling at Augusta, Georgia, and the forces at Charleston.[213]

Foragers ranged on every side of the main columns and pillaged and burned their way through South Carolina, tearing up railroad tracks behind them. They were trailed by hundreds of freedmen and refugees. Source: Library of Congress

Beauregard urged the evacuation of Charleston to avoid one of the South's few remaining armies being besieged.

Federals had been camping on Simms' Woodlands plantation in Bamberg since February 8, but they moved out on February 12.[214] Soon after the main troops left the area, the house was plundered and destroyed, and the livestock and forage stolen, but as disinformation, word was spread that stragglers or one of Simms' slaves had set the fire. Only the small brick outbuilding where Simms did much of his writing is still standing on his plantation, which is still owned by his descendants.

Simms was not living at the plantation when Sherman's troops came through because he was co-editor of the *Daily South Carolinian* in Columbia along with Henry Timrod, who fled the city before Sherman's arrival. From his newspaper office near the State House in Columbia, Simms waited in anguish as he described the passage of Sherman's troops from the Low Country up through the area in Bamberg where his plantation was located.

"No language can describe nor can any catalogue furnish an adequate detail of the wide-spread destruction of homes and property," he wrote. "Granaries were emptied, and where the grain was not carried off, it was strewn to waste under the feet of the cavalry or consigned to the fire which consumed the dwelling. The negroes were robbed equally with the whites of food and clothing. The roads were covered with butchered cattle, hogs, mules and the costliest furniture.... Horses were ridden into the houses. People were forced from their beds, to permit the search after hidden treasures."[215]

The heads of all of Sherman's columns reached the Edgefield Road on February 11, and the Seventeenth Corps turned to the right against Orangeburg. The bridge across the Edisto was gone, and Blair sent Mower's division to a spot four or five miles below the town to cross. Even though a pontoon bridge was laid, the men had to wade through waist-high water.[216] Sherman's men continued to march, but still hampered by rain, were forced to corduroy many of the roads with logs so wagons could pass. On February 12, about 600 Confederates occupied rifle pits and manned a small battery on the opposite side of the Edisto River. The Confederates had broken the bridge, and the river was deep and impassible. The skirmish and damaged bridge halted the advance of the right wing of the Federal Army commanded by Sherman, but Smith's soldiers repaired the bridge and Sherman was the first to cross over. Outflanked by a larger force, the Confederates were forced to withdraw toward Columbia.[217]

Entering Orangeburg, the Federals destroyed the railroad and depot and burned "a good deal of cotton"[218] and much of the city. As Sherman's troops were burning Orangeburg, Sherman was blaming the nearest Confederates and claiming that his men were putting out the fire and saving what was left of Orangeburg. "By and before the time either (General Manning F.) Force's or Giles A. Smith's skirmishers entered the place, several stores were on fire, and I am sure that some of the towns-people told me that a Jew merchant had set fire to his own cotton and store, and from this the fire had spread," Sherman said. "This, however, was soon put out, and the

Sherman's troops destroyed the railroad tracks in their path through Georgia and the Carolinas. The rails were heated and twisted into "Sherman's neckties," mounds of iron that could not be reset as rail lines.
Source: Library of Congress

Seventeenth Corps (General Blair) occupied the place during the night."[219]

Sherman established his headquarters that one night in the home of Judge Thomas W. Glover.[220] Even though Glover had signed the Ordinance of Secession, Sherman left a guard at the house so that it would not be destroyed.[221]

After the capture and destruction of most of Orangeburg, Sherman's troops marched rapidly, meeting almost no opposition from the Confederates until they approached the Little Congaree Creek (a tributary of the Congaree River), a broad tributary of the main Congaree about eight miles below Columbia.

The head of the 15th Corps, Woods' division, reached Thom's Creek, a stream below Congaree Creek located about 12 miles below the city, and the Little Congaree. Confederates defended the north side of Congaree Creek until the afternoon of Wednesday, February 15.[222] Within hours, the Confederates fell back across the Little Congaree, setting fire to the small bridge[223] and taking a stand on a high hill three miles from the creek.[224]

During the night, the Confederate battery shelled Woods' division in camp, killing and wounding several Federals. When Hood had berated Sherman for shelling Atlanta without notice, Sherman had said, "I was not bound by the laws of war to give notice of the shelling of Atlanta, a 'fortified town, with magazines, arsenals, foundries and public stores;' you were bound to take notice. See the books."[225] But when Confederates shelled one of his camps at night without warning on the bank of the Congaree outside Columbia, he angrily said, "This provoked me much at the time, for it was wanton mischief.... I have always contended that I would have been justified in retaliating for this unnecessary act of war, but did not, though I always characterized it as it deserved."[226]

At early dawn, the Federals were again on the move and before 9 a.m. on Thursday, February 16, the western bank of the Congaree River was in their possession, and troops could see Columbia from the base of the burned out Congaree (Gervais Street) bridge.[227]

7 'THE PANIC WAS REALLY FRIGHTFUL'

The odds of force against the Confederates were too vast for any valor or generalship to make head against it; and yet, ... the hope was held out to the people, in many quarters, that the city could be saved.

—William Gilmore Simms

Henry Timrod, the Poet Laureate of the South, was co-editor with William Gilmore Simms of the Daily South Carolinian in 1864 and 1865. Even though Timrod was terminally ill with tuberculosis, he was a war correspondent for three months for the Charleston (S.C.) Mercury. He wrote some of his best poetry during the war and died in 1867 at the age of 39. He is buried with his only child Willie at Trinity Episcopal Cathedral. This portrait is in the Walker Local History Room of the Richland Library, Columbia, S.C.
Photo by Pat McNeely.

Sherman's troops had been 21 miles from Columbia when he issued orders on February 13 for all columns to head for the capital city. The Federals had picked up a rebel officer on the road who had confessed that nothing was left in Columbia except Beauregard and Hampton with Hampton's cavalry.

"The fact was that General Hardee, in Charleston, took it for granted that we were after Charleston," Sherman said. "The rebel troops in Augusta supposed they were 'our objective;' so they abandoned poor Columbia to the care of Hampton's cavalry, which was confused by the rumors that poured in on it, so that both Beauregard and Wade Hampton, who were in Columbia, seem to have lost their heads."[228]

Until that day, most inhabitants thought the movement on Columbia was but a feint and that the bulk of Sherman's army was preparing for a descent upon Charleston, Simms wrote. But everything changed on Monday, February 13, when the Federal army reached a point in Lexington District, ten miles above Jeffcoat's plantation that was no more than 15 miles from Columbia.[229]

Troops consisting of the mounted men of Hampton, Wheeler and Butler skirmished with Sherman's men so close by that Simms could hear the Federal cannon "sound more heavily upon our ears," he said.

"We were but too certainly assured of the hopelessness of the struggle. The odds of force against the Confederates were too vast for any valor or generalship to make head against it; and yet,... the hope was held out to the people, in many quarters, that the city could be saved."[230]

After frequent reports were received about the intentions of "Tecump" and the promises made to the soldiers as to the license that would be allowed them when they captured the capital of South Carolina, the owner of the *Daily South Carolinian* had decided to remove the printing material to the upper part of the state.

Mayor Thomas Jefferson Goodwyn surrendered the city of Columbia to Sherman's troops. Goodwyn is frequently misidentified but this portrait belonged to his great-granddaughter Caroline Legare Judson. Oil portrait by William Harrison Scarborough circa 1835-1840. Courtesy of Caroline Legare Judson and the South Caroliniana Library at the University of South Carolina, Columbia, S.C.

The owner, Felix Gregory de Fontaine, was the South's most well-known and respected war correspondent and had been a reporter before the war for the *New York Herald* and during the war for the *Charleston Courier*. He owned the *Daily South Carolinian* and had hired Simms and Timrod as co-editors of his newspaper.[231]

Still in Richmond when Sherman captured Savannah, de Fontaine had decided that Sherman was headed for Columbia. He had returned to South Carolina in early January 1865 to warn of Sherman's inevitable approach and to hurriedly ship most of his newspaper material and equipment to Chester. His warnings went unheeded, and with the sound of cannon in his ears, de Fontaine left Columbia on February 14 on the last train carrying civilians out of Columbia before Sherman's troops advanced on the city.[232] His wife and newborn baby were with him, and he left the co-editors of his newspaper with enough type and supplies to continue to work. Timrod, who was dying of tuberculosis, fled as Sherman's troops approached the city, but Simms stayed in town and became an important eye-witness to the devastation that was to come.

Columbia was placed under martial law on Wednesday, February 15, under the direction of General E. M. Law, assisted by Goodwyn and Captains W. B. Stanley and John McKenzie, who were also city aldermen.[233]

Columbia Mayor Thomas Jefferson Goodwyn said, "On the 16th February, 1865, they commenced shelling the City from the opposite side of the river without any notice, or demand of surrender; it created much confusion amongst our Citizens." Goodwyn said the shelling demolished the steps to his house, which was located at Gervais and Sumter streets, "whilst my family was there; this shelling continued nearly all day."[234]

Captain David Conyngham, who was one of Sherman's aides and a reporter for the *New York Herald*, wrote: "A section was placed close to the bridge, so as to sweep the streets of the city, which were crowded with soldiers, citizens, and wagons, clearing out of the town. The shells soon burst among them, making them file right and left in double quick time." He reported that the 12th Missouri battery and the 17th corps took up a position on a hill across from Columbia and opened fire on the trains that were leaving the depot. "We were within five hundred yards of the city, which was situated on a rising bluff on the other side of the river, so that we could smash it to pieces in a short time by bringing sufficient artillery to bear on it."

Sherman's troops expected every moment that the city would be surrendered "for it now lay hopelessly in our power," Conyngham wrote.[235] Shells peppered the town; the new capitol building was struck five times,[236] Simms said, "yet we hear of only two persons killed—on the hospital square, and another near the South Carolina Railroad Depot."

The 19th Missouri and 7th Illinois reached Saluda Factory, which was located on the west side of today's Riverbanks Zoo in the Botanical Gardens, where the ruins can still be seen today. The three-story granite Saluda Factory, which by then was called Columbia Mills, was the only company manufacturing wool products in South Carolina. The factory had produced "jerseys" (knitted wool), "jeans," a type of twilled cotton in both stripes and white, and "plains," a kind of plain flannel cloth.[237]

"Federal skirmishers occupied the windows facing the river and were exchanging shots with the Rebels, who lay concealed among the bushes and timber on the other side," Nichols said.[238] He said

The old Saluda Factory was located on the west side of today's Riverbanks Zoo, where the ruins can still be seen. Courtesy of the South Caroliniana Library at the University of South Carolina, Columbia, S.C.

dirty wooden shanties were built on the river bank a few hundred feet above the factory, and "rotten steps led to foul and close passage-ways, filled with broken crockery, dirty pots and pans... where old women and ragged children lolled lazily in the sunshine."[239]

Nichols said the men had been expecting to find some good-looking women at the factory and were disappointed with the 250 "unkempt, frowzy, ragged, dirty, and altogether ignorant and wretched" workers who were hurrying through the building, "tearing the cloth from the looms, and filling bags with bales of yarn to be 'toted' home, as they phrase it."[240]

The Charlotte railroad depot in Columbia was crowded with people and luggage as residents tried to flee, but no civilians could leave the city after February 15 because the governments of the state and the Confederacy absorbed all means of conveyance. "Transportation about the city could not be had, save by a rich or

The ruins of the Saluda Factory are located in the Botanical Gardens of the Riverbanks Zoo in Columbia. Photo by Pat McNeely

favored few," Simms said.[241] Hardee was still in Charleston on February 15, and was being told by President Davis to hold Charleston as long as prudent before evacuating. Hardee refused to evacuate Charleston and head for Columbia, so Beauregard told the mayor that he could only hold Columbia two or three days longer.[242]

Hardee's troops began belatedly and reluctantly withdrawing from Charleston and Fort Sumter, which had been reduced to rubble, but it was too late to help Columbia so he headed for Chester.[243] Union troops marched into Charleston the same day and took possession of Fort Sumter and the other forts and batteries. Hill, who

The Charlotte Railroad was located a block west of the campus of today's Benedict College. The last train out left on Thursday, February 16. Sherman and Mayor Thomas Jefferson Goodwyn strolled from the vicinity of the State House to this location on the afternoon of Friday, February 17, to visit one of Sherman's old friends. Adapted from an 1872 map. Source: Library of Congress

had left Augusta on February 13, could not reach Columbia in time either, so he also turned toward Chester.

On Wednesday, February 15, Slocum's Army of Georgia advanced. The army had been created from the 20th Corps and the 14th Corps from the Army of the Cumberland, which served as the left wing in Sherman's March to the Sea and the Carolinas Campaign. The left wing advanced toward Columbia, marching along a route near Red Bank Creek toward Lexington.

Slocum's troops, who were led by skirmishers, were delayed by Wheeler's cavalry, who clashed with them briefly along a creek in what became known as the Skirmish at Red Bank Creek.[244] After the Confederates withdrew through Lexington, two miles north, elements of the 20th Corps occupied the town. Kilpatrick's cavalry burned much of Lexington before the left wing advanced toward Winnsboro, leaving Lexington a "blackened ruin."[245] As Sherman's troops passed through the Lexington area, troops burned St. Stephen's Lutheran Church, which had been founded in 1830. It was the earliest church in Lexington.[246]

The week before Sherman's troops approached Columbia, Dr. Joseph LeConte, professor of chemistry and geology at South Carolina College, had been deciding what to do about the chemical laboratory he was operating on campus that was supplying medicine for the Confederates, and the Nitre Bureau. "The indefatigable Sherman was close by, and I knew not how soon I might be compelled to run," LeConte would write later. "The next week was an anxious one for all of us, and its memory is burned into my brain. The enemy, swearing vengeance against South Carolina, the cradle of secession, approached step by step; consternation and panic-flight of women and children in front and a blackened ruin behind."[247]

LeConte received orders from the Confederate administration to send the chemical laboratory to Richmond, and, after packing for several days, shipped the boxes by rail on February 15. The depot was crowded with people trying to get away, women and children pleading to be taken aboard the cars. "The panic was really frightful," he said, "but still I strove to remain calm, for, though both our first and second lines of defense had been carried and the booming of the enemy's guns sounded ever nearer and nearer, the various authorities confidently said there was no real danger—Hardee's army corps would surely come in time."[248]

However, on his way home that night LeConte met a wagon train fully half a mile long, "rumbling slowly and softly through the silent and deserted streets toward the Charlotte depot, as if stealing away in the dark," he said. It was a Confederate army-train, and "the solemn rumbling as it dragged its slow length along smote painfully on my heart. For the first time my hopes utterly gave way, and, I thought, 'Columbia is doomed!'"[249]

And while Confederate troops were preparing to evacuate the city on the night of Wednesday, February 15, Sherman camped on the "nearest dry ground" behind the Little Congaree, a few miles west of Columbia, where he would write the order to govern the troops while occupying the city.[250]

Dr. Joseph LeConte manufactured medicine for the Confederacy on the South Carolina College campus. He was also in charge of the Niter Bureau, which manufactured niter for gunpowder. After the war, he became a professor at the University of California at Berkeley where he was co-founder of the Sierra Club with John Muir. Courtesy of the South Caroliniana Library at the University of South Carolina, Columbia, S.C.

8 'LEAVING COLUMBIA IN THE HANDS OF THE ENEMY'

By daylight, few remained in the city who were not resigned to the necessity of seeing the tragedy played out.

—*William Gilmore Simms*

The Confederate military authorities had at last confessed to Dr. LeConte that they could not hold Columbia and advised him to save what Niter Bureau stores and medicines he could. Desperately trying to save valuables, manuscripts, lecture notes, niter and other government property, Le Conte left his family behind on the South Carolina College campus and set out at 6 a.m. Thursday, February 16, with two wagons, two carts and a buggy, all heavily loaded, to head to Alston, 25 miles north of Columbia. He was planning to cross the Broad River toward Edgefield.

"That was the saddest night of my life," LeConte said. "Our imperative duty was to save, if possible, the government property in our care, and it would have been worse than useless for us to have remained, for as we were all officers, we should certainly

Confederates burned the Congaree (Gervais Street) Bridge just before Sherman's troops arrived. Courtesy of the South Caroliniana Library at the University of South Carolina, Columbia, S.C.

have been taken prisoners. And yet it was hard to leave in the hands of the enemy all that we loved most tenderly."[251] As he plodded out of the city, he did not know that Sherman would order Slocum to also turn north with the left wing toward Alston to cross the Broad River at the same place LeConte was headed.[252]

By the time Sherman arrived at the west end of the Congaree (Gervais Street) Bridge, the superstructure had been burned and only the stone piers were still standing. U.S. Colonel Ross, chief of artillery, 15th Corps, had ordered up Captain Francis De Grass's battery on the west side of the river directly across from Columbia. DeGress had a section of his 20-pound Parrott guns unlimbered at the base of the burned-out bridge.

Troops were also shelling the city from batteries on a hill off modern day Highway 378 in West Columbia. Shells were being lobbed toward the Arsenal, which is now part of the Governor's Mansion, and the new State House.[253]

One of the shells aimed at the new State House passed through the old State House, and one shell fell into a passing buggy, which was, according to James G. Gibbes, the last vehicle to leave the city.[254]

When Sherman asked DeGress why he was firing into the city, he said he thought there was a large force of infantry concealed on the opposite bank.

Sherman ordered him not to fire into the town anymore, but he consented to DeGress bursting a few shells near the depot "to scare away the negroes who were appropriating the bags of corn and meal which we wanted, also to fire three shots at the unoccupied State-House."[255]

"No summons for surrender had been made; no warning of any kind was given," Simms said.[256]

Sherman was heavily criticized after the war for firing into the city without warning and without demanding surrender.

However, even though Simms reported that two people had been killed, Sherman would say, "Although this matter of firing into Columbia has been the subject of much abuse and investigation, I have yet to hear of any single person having been killed in Columbia by our cannons that day."[257]

Confederates had burned the Congaree (Gervais Street) Bridge by the time Sherman arrived at the west end of the bridge where he found his soldiers had unlimbered a section of their 20-pound Parrott guns at the base of the burned-out bridge and were firing into the town. Sherman decided that the Congaree was too broad to cross on pontoons at the Congaree Bridge and sent his troops north to cross the Saluda and Broad Rivers into Columbia. The left wing was sent north to Alston to cross the Broad River and head for Winnsboro. Adapted from an 1872 map of Columbia. **Source: Library of Congress**

The Confederates were in full retreat out of Columbia on Thursday, February 16, including Governor Andrew Gordon Magrath and a large group of officials who took one of the last trains toward Union, where he would establish the temporary capital of the state.

However, Beauregard did not relinquish his command to Hampton until Thursday evening. "On that night I was notified by Gen Beauregard that the City would be evacuated by his forces early the next morning (before daylight)," Goodwyn said.[258]

Gibbes said that by then Hampton's command "did not exceed eight hundred men."[259]

Beauregard planned to head north towards Ridgeway, which was 20 miles away, where he would establish his headquarters February 17-19 in front of the Century House on Railroad Avenue in Fairfield County. He would telegraph news of the military evacuation of Columbia to Lee before moving to Winnsboro on February 19.[260]

Sherman had decided that the Congaree River was too broad to cross with pontoons near the burned-out Congaree (Gervais Street) Bridge and issued orders for the troops to head north and cross the Saluda and the Broad rivers into Columbia. Hazen's men had already found that the bridge over the Saluda River had been burned, and he ordered his men to cross over in pontoon boats and on rafts.

Sherman's troops crossing the Saluda River. Source: Library of Congress

Wheeler had wanted a concentration of troops on the Saluda River, but Beauregard had met with him personally on February 14 and ordered him to cross the Broad River and picket the Saluda from its mouth north for 10 miles and the Congaree below the city. Wheeler and his men had been in place early on Wednesday, February 15, but his force was inadequate.

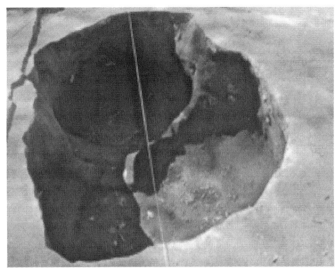

Sherman discovered that Federal prisoners who had been in Camp Sorghum on the west bank of the Congaree had dug holes like this to stay warm. These holes were excavated in 2014 at Camp Asylum on the grounds of the State Hospital, which is where the prisoners were moved in October 1864. Photo by Pat McNeely

As Wheeler had surmised, all of Sherman's force was directed upon the Saluda, which was narrow with high banks.

"After sharp skirmishing, we managed to get a few men across the river in boats," Nichols said. "Usually our foragers have the advance, but in this instance, the skirmishers had all the fun to themselves."[261]

The concentration of Howard's artillery and infantry quickly gave the Federals control of both banks, and a large body of troops was thrown across the Saluda.[262] By nightfall on February 16, Sherman's troops had rafted or pontooned across the Saluda and charged across the tongue of land that separates it from the Broad River.[263] Wheeler concentrated his available force, but was only able to stop the Federals briefly as they advanced toward the Broad River Bridge, a distance of not more than a mile from their crossing point on the Saluda.[264]

Sherman camped on the night of February 16 near Camp Sorghum, a prisoner-of-war camp located on the Congaree River, just off modern-day Highway 378. The camp had been vacated when the

1,200 Federal prisoners had been moved on October 4, 1864, to the prisoner-of-war camp on the grounds at the Asylum (the South Carolina State Hospital) at the east end of Upper Boundary (Elmwood) Avenue.[265]

Sherman said he could see the "mud-hovels and holes in the ground which our prisoners had made to shelter themselves from the winter's cold and the summer's heat."[266] The prisoners in Columbia had been shipped to Charlotte during the previous two days, but sixty of them had escaped and hidden in spaces under the floors and between the ceiling boards and roof of the Asylum until Sherman's troops arrived.

Under cover of sharpshooters on the top floor of the three-story granite Saluda Factory, Sherman's troops finished crossing the Saluda River and burned the factory behind them.[267] "It was sad to see in Saluda groups of female operatives weeping and wringing their hands in agony, as they saw the factory, their only means of support, in flames," Conyngham wrote.[268]

The head of the 15th Corps reached the Broad River just in time to find the bridge in flames, and the 17th Crops was right behind. Butler's cavalry had just passed over into Columbia, setting the bridge on fire behind them. The head of Slocum's left wing and the cavalry had also reached the same point, but Sherman had ordered them to

Sherman's army crossing the Broad River on a pontoon bridge. *Source: Library of Congress*

turn north to cross the Broad River 25 miles[269] north of Columbia at Alston.

Federals started laying a pontoon bridge,[270] which, according to Columbia historian David Brinkman, was upstream of today's Broad River Road Bridge and across a small island.[271]

The direct movement on Columbia began at 3 a.m. Friday, February 17, when a brigade of infantry was pushed across and gained a firm footing on the east bank.[272] Stone pushed over silently in canvas bottom pontoon boats, two miles above the city, and he and his men lay on their arms until dawn, carrying everything before them.[273]

In the early morning hours before dawn on Friday, February 17, a terrific explosion shook the ground in Columbia like an earthquake. The South Carolina Railroad Depot (the Charleston railroad) was accidentally blown up, according to Simms and Goodwyn. The depot was bounded by Gervais, Pendleton, Lincoln and Wayne streets and was four blocks east of the Gervais Street Bridge.

A larger quantity of powder in the depot had been ignited by the careless use of lights by a band of plunderers, many of whom were killed by the explosion. The plunderers had broken into the depot and, in order to better see the contents of the depot, had fired a train of powder leading to some kegs of powder.

The South Carolina Railroad, also called the Charleston Railroad, at Gervais and Lincoln streets, was accidentally blown up in the early morning hours of Friday, February 17. The Federals had already crossed the Broad River by then. Source: Library of Congress

The ruins of the freight depot of the S.C. Railroad were visible from the west side of the Congaree River just south of the spot where Sherman's troops were beginning to cross the Saluda and Broad rivers into the city. Courtesy of the South Caroliniana Library at the University of South Carolina, Columbia, S.C.

Since some of Sherman's foragers had already crossed the rivers by then, they were most likely among those who had been killed. Simms was not sure how many people were killed or injured: "The number of persons destroyed is variously estimated, from seventeen to fifty," he said. "It is probable that not more than thirty-five suffered, but the actual number perishing is unascertained." [274]

After the explosion, Goodwyn "immediately went to the City Hall and was about to raise the white flag, but Hampton requested that it should not be done until he gave the order.[275]

The commissary and quartermaster stores were thrown open to the public after the early morning explosion and the contents had been cast into the streets and given to the people. "Wheeler's cavalry also shared largely of this plunder, and several of them might be seen, bearing off huge bales upon their saddles," Simms wrote.[276]

However, even though Wheeler's men shared in the plunder, the men carrying off bales on their saddles were more likely marauders traveling under Wheeler's name, as Wilson had said. When Wheeler reached Wayne County, North Carolina, he heard that Columbians were accusing his men of pillaging and plundering.

He issued a statement on April 3 protesting the charges of depredations that were said to have been caused by them and saying that "the great bulk of outrages were perpetrated by organized bands of lawless men who took advantage of our presence to plunder citizens under our name, and this at the very time when our whole command was engaged day after day in fighting and impeding the march of Sherman's column, and that nearly, if not quite all, of the property taken or impressed by us was taken by order of the department commander, and would have fallen, as all left by us did fall, into the hands of the enemy, thereby contributing to the ability of Sherman to accomplish the object of his campaign. And all property even thus taken has, upon application, been returned without a murmur."[277]

Mayor Goodwyn surrendered the city to Sherman's troops at the corner of Beaufort Street and River Drive just north of the Upper Boundary (Elmwood Avenue) where this stone marks the spot. Photo by Pat McNeely

Wheeler's men had skirmished with the Federals until he received a note at 7:45 a.m. from General C. L. Stevenson saying that the enemy had crossed the Broad River to an island formed by the river and a slough in their front and would soon be crossing to the mainland.[278] By daylight, few remained in the city "who were not resigned to the necessity of seeing the tragedy played out," Simms said.

After everyone who could had fled, probably less than two-thirds of the population was left, "the larger proportion being females and children and negroes."[279]

The stressed mayor of Columbia said, "About 8 o'clock that morning he (Hampton) rode up to the Hall and said the flag could be raised. He then advised me where to proceed to the Northern Army and how to proceed. Nearby us there was some cotton piled in the streets, and I think it was him that advised me to have a guard put over it, for fear that if it got on fire it might endanger the City."[280] Beauregard and Hampton left orders that the wet cotton, which had been prepared for shipment out of Columbia to be burned elsewhere, should not be burned in the city. The orders were issued to Captain Rawlins Lowndes, then acting as Hampton's adjutant, and Butler, who was with the rear squadron of the cavalry and who said that

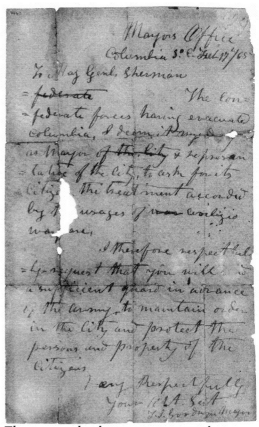

The surrender letter was passed down through generations of the family of Mayor Thomas Jefferson Goodwyn. Courtesy of his great granddaughter Caroline Legare Judson and the South Caroliniana Library at the University of South Carolina, Columbia, S.C.

Hampton's order was communicated to the entire division "and was strictly observed."[281]

Immediately after parting with Hampton on Friday, February 17, Goodwyn, accompanied by city Aldermen McKenzie, John Stork and Orlando Z. Bates, rode in a carriage bearing a white flag towards the Broad River Bridge Road to meet Sherman's army.[282] Arriving at the forks of the Winnsboro Road, they discovered that Wheeler's soldiers were still busy with their guns to give the main army all possible advantages of a start in their retreat. Stone's brigade had advanced to within two miles of Columbia when Goodwyn and his delegation arrived in a carriage at 9 a.m. or 10 a.m. to surrender the town.[283] Goodwyn and his deputation found a column of Federals from the 15th Corps some distance beyond the Upper Boundary (Elmwood Avenue). "Coln Stone (then acting as Brig Gen) was in command, he promised safety to our City until Gen Sherman arrived; he sent my billet of surrender across the river to the Genl," Goodwyn said.[284] Stone took his seat with them in the carriage at the intersection of Beaufort Street and River Road. A Surrender Stone marks the spot where Goodwyn presented his letter of surrender:

Mayors Office

Columbia So. C. Feb 17th/65

To Maj Genl. Sherman

The Confederate forces having evacuated Columbia, I deem it my duty as Mayor and representative of the City, to ask for its citizens the treatment accorded by the usage of civilized warfare.

I therefore respectfully request that you will send a sufficient guard in advance of the Army to maintain order in the city and protect the persons and property of the citizens.

Very Respectfully,

Your Servt

T. J. Goodwyn, Mayor

Stone said, "The mayor met us near the city and made a formal 'unconditional surrender.' I had refused any other; but upon his accepting, at once promised protection for all private property." Goodwyn also said that Stone "promised safety to our City until Gen Sherman arrived; he sent my billet of surrender across the river to the Genl," Goodwyn wrote.

On the west bank, surrounded by his generals, Sherman watched from a high bluff overlooking the rivers as the drama unfolded. From his vantage point across the wide Congaree, Sherman "could see the unfinished State-House, a handsome granite structure, and the ruins of the railroad depot, which were still smouldering.

"Occasionally a few citizens or cavalry could be seen running across the streets, and quite a number of negroes were seemingly busy in carrying off bags of grain or meal, which were piled up near the burned depot."[285]

Sherman alternated between being calm and nervous. "There was General Sherman, now pacing up and down in the midst of the group all the time, with an unlit cigar in his mouth, and now and then abruptly halting to speak to some of the generals around him," Conyngham wrote. "Again he would sit down, whittle a stick, and soon nervously start up to resume his walk. Above all the men I have ever met, that strange face of his is the hardest to be read. It is a sealed book even to his nearest friends."[286]

Sherman was sitting on a log with Howard watching the men lay the pontoon bridge across the Broad River when the messenger arrived at 9 a.m. or 10 a.m.[287] from Stone on the other side, saying that the mayor of Columbia had surrendered the city and asking for orders.[288] "I simply remarked to General Howard that he had his orders, to let Colonel Stone go on into the city, and that we would follow as soon as the bridge was ready," he said.[289]

Sherman had written the order for the government of Columbia while he was camped at Congaree Creek. The order was simple and in no way resembled the generous terms and protection provided in Savannah. Dated February 16, General Order No. 26 said: "General Howard will cross the Saluda and Broad Rivers as near their mouths as possible, occupy Columbia, destroy the public buildings, railroad property, manufacturing and machine shops; but will spare libraries, asylums and private dwellings. He will then move on to Winnsboro, destroying en route utterly that section of the railroad. He will also cause all bridges, trestles, water-tanks, and depots on the railroad back to the Wateree to be burned, switches broken, and such other destruction as he can find time to accomplish consistent with proper celerity."[290]

Although the order specified that libraries and private dwellings should be spared, Sherman included instructions for "such other destruction as (Howard) can find time to accomplish consistent with proper celerity," which meant that Sherman had again provided enough leeway for his men, particularly the foragers, to continue pillaging, plundering and burning.

9 THE DOOMED CITY

For I must tell you, my sister, that Columbia is a doomed city.
—Sherman's officer sent to protect the Ursuline Convent

While the mayor was surrendering the city, Hampton and his remaining cavalry, which had lingered until nearly 10 a.m. on Friday, February 17, headed north to Ridgeway, according to Simms. Scattered groups of Wheeler's command hovered about the Federal army at their entrance into the town until almost 11 a.m. when Wheeler was driven to the junction of the Broad River and Winnsboro roads.[291]

In the seven weeks since Sherman had entered South Carolina, Wheeler had been the primary defense mounted in the state.

His men had hovered close to

General John "Black Jack" Logan, who was known for his hostility and desire to destroy property, was commander of the 15th Army Corps, which was chosen by Sherman to enter the city. Logan had a reputation for being the most destructive officer in Sherman's army.
Source: Library of Congress

Sherman's columns, inflicting losses in killed, wounded and prisoners. Wheeler had destroyed every bridge in Sherman's path and had obstructed every road. Now Wheeler watched helplessly as

Sherman's troops advanced on Columbia.[292] Logan's 15th Corps, which entered the city first, was the part of Sherman's forces with a reputation for the greatest destruction. "Yes, sir," Howard would say in testimony in 1872. "Part of the 15th corps were rather remarkable, prior to this campaign, for the destruction of property; they had been under orders to do it more than other forces." Howard had first noticed Logan's "disposition to destroy property, and the manifestation of hostile feeling" at Beaufort.[293]

Even knowing Logan's predisposition for destruction, Howard said he had not believed that Columbia would be burned because "I thought we had sufficient power over our force to prevent anything of the kind, if anything of the kind was meditated, of which I had no evidence."[294]

The 13th Iowa Regiment of the 17th Corps is depicted as charging south down Richardson (Main) Street to raise the Union flag on the new State House in Columbia. However, the 17th Corps actually planted regimental flags that were replaced with the Union flag by Stone and the 15th Corps. Courtesy of the South Caroliniana Library at the University of South Carolina, Columbia, S.C.

The leading divisions of the Fifteenth Corps who marched into Columbia made their camps east of the city, generally from about where Benedict University is located today and east out Trenholm Road and down through today's Five Points and south. The rest of Howard's command, the 17th Corps, were not supposed to enter the city at first, but were to cross directly over to the Winnsboro Road and toward the pontoon bridge at Broad River, which was about four miles north of the city, where they made camp.[295] Simms and James Gibbes said that as many as 20,000 soldiers were camped east of the city. Goodwyn, who believed that the city would be protected, was accompanied back to the city about 11 a.m. by Stone and his men.[296]

The head of Stone's column, which consisted of Goodwyn and his deputation riding in a carriage flying a U.S. flag, reached the City Center on Main Street at Washington Street followed by the corps. On their way into the city, the carriage was stopped and the officer was informed that a large body of Confederate cavalry was flanking them. "Colonel Stone said to the Mayor, 'We shall hold you responsible for this!'

Federals came into Columbia down River Road (upper left) that crossed the Upper Boundary cross street (Elmwood Avenue) and became Richardson (Main) Street. Source: Library of Congress

"The Mayor explained that the road leading to Winnsboro, by which the Confederates were retreating, ran nearly parallel for a short distance with the River Road, which accounted for the apparent flanking," Simms said.

"Two officers, who arrived in Columbia ahead of the deputation (having crossed the river at a point directly opposite the city,) were fired upon by one of Wheeler's cavalry," Simms said. "We are particular in mentioning this fact, as we learn that, subsequently, the incident was urged as a justification of the sack and burning of the city."[297]

General Oliver Howard was commander of the right wing that entered the city of Columbia. Howard would become director of the Freedmen's Bureau after the war and founder of Howard University in Washington, D.C.
Source: Library of Congress

In a letter Stone wrote after the war to the editor of the *Chicago Tribune*, he described his entry into Columbia. "As we entered one of the principal streets, the sidewalks were lined with negroes of every age, sex and condition, holding in their arms vessels of every conceivable size and shape, filled with almost every conceivable kind of liquor... Others were offering wines, champagne, etc. from original packages, tin cups, crocks, etc. Officers were at once reminded that their men, considering their fatigue of the past few days, their sharp fight of the morning, their loss of sleep, and no food for the past 24 hours, were in no condition to drink much liquor."[298]

Stone's description of the entry into the city was verified by Howard in testimony and cross-examination in 1872 when Howard said he was told when he arrived in the city a couple of hours later about the "pails of whiskey along the ranks" from which Stone's men "drank with dippers out of the pails" when they arrived at Main

Street.[299]   Stone quickly posted Federal guards throughout the city and rode south down Richardson (Main) Street to plant the national colors on the unfinished State House.[300] Soldiers from the 17th Corps, who were supposed to be heading north of town, had already reached the State House and planted regimental flags, which were replaced with the Union flag.

Stone was absent from the brigade about an hour placing the Federal flag on the State House, and "when I rejoined my command found a great number of the men drunk," he said.

"It was discovered that this was caused by hundreds of negroes who swarmed the streets on the approach of the troops and gave them all kinds of liquors from buckets, bottles, demijohns, &c. The men had slept none the night before, and but little the night before that, and many of them had no supper the night before, and none of them breakfast that morning, hence the speedy effect of the liquor. I forthwith ordered all the liquor destroyed, and saw fifteen barrels destroyed within five minutes after the order had been given."[301]

Stone said Woods now sent word to him to guard the private property of the citizens and take possession of all the public buildings. "I did so immediately upon receipt of the order, distributing my five regiments throughout the city and appointing Lieutenant-Colonel Jenkins, Thirty-first Iowa, provost-marshal," Stone said.[302]

"A great many drunken men were now showing themselves in the streets from, I should think, every regiment of our corps, the Seventeenth Corps, and some even from General Kilpatrick's cavalry. My command was so scattered throughout the city I found it necessary to have a stronger guard, and therefore applied through my acting assistant adjutant-general to Brevet Major-General Woods twice, once in writing, for one or two more regiments for patrolling the city, but received no re-enforcements."[303]

In their intoxicated condition, the troops had barely reached the head of Main Street at Upper Boundary (Elmwood Avenue) when the work of pillaging began, Simms said.[304] Even though Federal guards were quickly posted throughout the city, Simms said, "In a number of cases, the guards were the most active plunderers;

Sherman's troops entered from the north end of Columbia and poured down Richardson (Main) Street, drinking from pails of liquor along the way and robbing and pillaging the houses and stores. More than three-fifths of the town was burned. The town market (10) on Assembly Street was destroyed, as was the jail (9) at Washington and Assembly and the City Hall (11), which was at the corner of Washington and Richardson (Main). Simms' newspaper office (14) was on Washington Street near Main. The First Baptist Church (20) survived and is facing Plain (Hampton) Street at Sumter Street across from Dr. Robert Gibbes' house (21), which was burned along with the Washington Street Methodist Church (22) at the corner of Washington and Marion. First Presbyterian (23) on Marion Street survived, but Mayor Thomas Jefferson Goodwyn's house (25) at Gervais and Sumter was burned. The old State House (27) burned, but the new State House (26) survived as did Trinity Episcopal Church (Cathedral) (28). Adapted from an 1872 map of Columbia. Source: Library of Congress

were quick to betray their trusts, abandon their posts, and bring their comrades in to join in the general pillage."[305]

The mayor concurred: "The soldiers in company with the negroes commenced breaking open houses and robbing before they

had been in 20 minutes; in many places at private houses the guard had no control."[306]

"Stores were broken open within the first hour after their arrival, and gold, silver, jewels and liquors, eagerly sought," Simms said. "The authorities, officers, soldiers, all, seemed to consider it a matter of course. And woe to him who carried a watch with gold chain pendant; or who wore a choice hat, or overcoat, or boots or shoes.

"He was stripped in the twinkling of an eye. It is computed that, from first to last, twelve hundred watches

James G. Gibbes
Courtesy of Gibbes' great-granddaughter Carolyn Gibbes White

were transferred from the pocket of their owners to those of the soldiers. Purses shared the same fate."[307]

Stone, who was the first officer on the scene, was not called upon to testify at the hearings in Washington in 1872 because Sherman said he "didn't know where (Stone) was." However, Stone immediately wrote a letter to the *Chicago Tribune* in which he explained that cotton was not burning when he entered the city.

He saw that the bales of cotton in the street had been cut open, and he did not see any cotton fires until about noon when he ordered his men to help extinguish a blaze near the center of the city. Stone said that no fires had occurred in any part of the city up to that time except for public buildings and the quartermasters' stores, which he said he believed had been fired by the enemy the day before his troops entered, "but which fire had not extended and did not extend to any other part of the city."[308]

The Reverend Peter Shand, who was the rector of Trinity Episcopal (Cathedral) Church for 50 years, said a row of bales of loosely packed cotton burned in the center of Main (or (Richardson Street), (apparently in front of the Congaree Hotel, on the southwest corner of Main street and Lady).

The cotton was in the middle of just part of the block with an interval of several feet between the bales and the pavement and houses on either side, he said.[309] The dirt streets were 100-feet wide in most places (although six streets were 150-feet wide) and muddy from the all-night rain, which meant that it would have taken at least 25 bales of cotton to stretch in a single row across any street.[310]

Bales of cotton, which were usually four feet wide, typically were tightly packed with metal straps and burlap and weighed about 400 pounds. Even when the straps and burlap were removed, cotton bales are usually still tightly packed and difficult to burn. The cotton bales in Columbia streets were soaked from an overnight rain but were cut open to burn more quickly. Accelerants might also have been used to burn the cotton, which otherwise could just smolder for days. Photo by Pat McNeely

The cotton was piled near the market on Assembly and Washington and on Richardson (Main) in front of the City Hall. The jail, which was also set on fire, was located at Washington and Assembly streets near the market. Adapted from an 1872 map of Columbia. Source: Library of Congress

"The bales were ragged and in bad order," he said. "This cotton was not fired or attempted to be fired, according to my knowledge, prior to the evacuation by the Confederate forces, and was not burning until after the troops of General Sherman took possession of the city on the afternoon of the 17th."[311]

As the soldiers poured into Columbia, The Reverend Shand said he was standing on the side pavement with several other citizens, watching a large number of soldiers, "who, in a condition of wild and joyous excitement were passing to and fro around the cotton—all or most of them with lighted pipes or cigars in their mouths.

"The wind was very high, and after a little while, I saw a bale at one end of the row become ignited, and immediately the flames spread until they extended the entire length," he said. "Efforts were made to extinguish them, but they raged with great fury and by one o'clock, the whole mass of cotton was in ashes and the fire put out without having been communicated to any of the neighboring buildings.

"The conflagration of the cotton was doubtless caused by the accidental falling upon it of sparks from a cigar or pipe. Indeed, there was nothing else to occasion it and our people could have had no part in producing it, for there was not one of them nearer to the bales than the sidewalk at the time of the occurrence."[312]

At about the same time, the jail was set on fire from within and all the prisoners escaped, Simms said.[313] The jail was near the corner of Assembly and Washington and directly behind City Hall. Soon after the jail fires started, a second cotton fire flared up.

Gibbes heard the fire alarm at about 1 p.m., and he hurried to Richardson (Main) street where he found about 60 bales of cotton that had been rolled into the center of the street and were on fire.

"As I approached it, I found a few men (citizens) had run out the Independent Engine from its house, near the market, not over one hundred yards from the burning cotton, and began playing on the fire," he said.[314]

The fire was soon extinguished but the citizens continued to spray water on the smoking bales till all signs of fire were gone.

"Not less than one thousand Federal soldiers were on the sidewalks looking on, but took no part at the fire until just as it was about all controlled, when a drunken soldier took his musket and plunged the bayonet into the hose pipe. Instantly a number of others joined in and with their bayonets soon cut the entire hose to pieces. Fortunately the fire was all over before this destruction of the hose. Before 2 p.m. all sign of the fire was over."[315]

The Reverend Shand said the only other place in town where there was any cotton in the streets was on a parallel street (probably

Assembly), but "the bales in this second row were fewer in number than that in the first, and, when I saw them in the afternoon, they were intact, and there were no other fires in the (downtown) city until after dark that I was aware of."[316] He said all the cotton fires set by the Federals that morning were out by 2 p.m.

Sherman had been still on the west side of the Broad River when the cotton and jail fires started on Main Street, and it was almost 11 a.m. before the pontoon bridges had been finished. But it

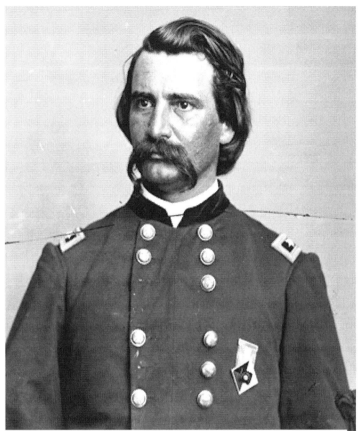

General John "Black Jack" Logan played a significant role in the burning of Columbia. His reputation for burning and destruction was well known, and even after Sherman issued orders on Saturday, February 18, to stop burning private property in Columbia, Logan was preparing to burn the Hampton-Preston House, which had been his headquarters. He was angry when Sherman gave the house to the Mother Superior after the Ursuline Convent was burned.
Source: Library of Congress

would be almost noon before Sherman, accompanied by Generals Howard, Logan, Woods and the 15th Corps, would cross the Broad River just north of Columbia to begin the occupation of Columbia.

As Sherman and Howard were entering the city, the 17th Corps began marching through northern Columbia without stopping and headed northeast to make their camps a few miles north of the city. Sherman and Howard both saw the cotton fires in the street that had been started by their own men before they arrived on the scene.

The first fires on Friday, February 17 at midday were in front of the City Hall (11) on Richardson (Main) Street and at the jail (35) on Washington Street near the market (10) on Assembly Street. The courthouse (33) once stood at Main and Washington streets. William Gilmore Simms saw the first fires started by the Federals from his office in the Daily South Carolinian (36) on Washington Street. Source: Adapted from an 1872 map of Columbia. Library of Congress.

"Side by side, Sherman and I entered the city and traversed the main streets," Howard said. "There was not much demonstration from the white people, but the negroes gave their usual exhibitions of delight, sometimes dancing upon the sidewalks, sometimes shouting and singing."[317]

Although Stone's entry into the city of Columbia had been marked by rampant pillaging and exuberant drinking, Sherman's arrival was orderly and controlled—at least until the troops were dismissed, according to Conyngham. *The New York Herald* reporter made no mention of seeing any fire as he described Sherman's entry into the city: "Our march through the city was so orderly that even the southerners began to bless their stars that the reign of terror was over, and that a reign of peace and security, like that at Savannah, was about to be inaugurated. Alas that the scenes of the night should mar so auspicious a beginning."[318]

The jail on Washington near Assembly streets was the first structure set on fire in Columbia—around noon on Friday, February 17. Courtesy of the South Caroliniana Library at the University of South Carolina, Columbia, S.C.

When Sherman described his trip along the same route that had been followed by Stone and Goodwyn into the city, he said the wind was up and cotton was burning near the market square, which was located on the west side of Richardson (Main) at Washington, just two blocks from the State House in the center of downtown Columbia. Flakes of cotton from the bales that had been cut open by the Federals were blowing through the air and lodging in trees so much that Sherman said it reminded him of a Northern snowstorm.[319]

"Near the market-square we found Stone's brigade halted, with arms stacked, and a large detail of his men, along with some citizens, engaged with an old fire-engine, trying to put out the fire in a long pile of burning cotton-bales...," Sherman said.

"I know that, to avoid this row of burning cotton-bales, I had to ride my horse on the sidewalk." The fires that Stone and his men were trying to extinguish with an old fire engine were the fires that had been set by the Federals before Sherman arrived and were the same fires described by Stone, Simms and the Reverend Shand. Hampton and Wheeler had been out of the city for more than two hours by then, but Sherman was quick to blame Confederates. "I was told (the cotton) had been fired by the rebel cavalry on withdrawing from the city that morning," he said.[320]

Howard described the same broken cotton bales on fire in the middle of the street with "soldiers and citizens" putting out the fire as they entered the city, but it would be eight hours before the downtown holocaust would begin.[321] He would later talk vaguely in his memoirs about cotton being set on fire by Confederates but he would also admit in later years that Sherman's troops had burned Columbia, but not on orders.[322]

In testimony in 1872, Howard admitted that no Confederate soldiers were left in Columbia when the fires started and a number of Federal soldiers were drunk. Sherman too had noticed his drunken soldiers as he rode into town; so, he rode back to the market-square and called Howard's attention to "several" of his men who "were evidently in liquor"[323] and ordered the division replaced.

Howard said he had "noticed that our own troops were unusually demonstrative in cheering for Sherman, and learned that traders and negroes had carried out buckets of whiskey to them wishing to please and pacify the men. The soldiers had worked all night and marched to Columbia without a breakfast. Numbers of Stone's brigade were thus excited and soon intoxicated."[324]

Howard immediately complied with Sherman's command, saying, "I ordered those that were drunk under guard immediately, and made every disposition necessary for the protection of property."[325] Although Sherman had ordered the replacement of the first regiment of drunken soldiers, the replacement division of soldiers "soon got as drunk as the first regiment that occupied the town," according to Captain Andrews.[326]

10 THE THREE-ROCKET SIGNAL

If you have anything you wish to save, take care of it at once, for before morning this d___d town will be in ashes—every house in it.
                                          —a Federal officer to William H. Orchard

If the entrance of Sherman's cavalcade into town and while on duty was indicative of admirable drill and discipline, that stopped the moment the troops were dismissed. "Then, whether by tacit permission or direct command, their whole deportment underwent a sudden and rapid change," Simms said.

The plundering and robberies, which had started that morning at about 11 a.m. when they reached the Market Hall in the center of town, continued without interruption throughout the day, Simms

Sherman entered the city at about noon and is shown here riding west on Lady Street with the First Presbyterian Church in the background. Cotton was blowing into the trees from slashed bales. Source: Library of Congress

reported.[327] Sherman recalled that he was on horseback when Goodwyn came walking up Main Street to meet him. The mayor was described by Sherman as "quite a respectable old gentleman who was extremely anxious to protect the interests of the citizens."[328]

The mayor said, "(Sherman) said he had received my letter and all would be right," and Goodwyn sent a servant with Sherman to the home of Blanton Duncan on Gervais and Henderson streets (where the Clarion Town House is today).

Goodwyn had procured a house for Sherman's Headquarters on Gervais Street that was just four blocks east of his own house. Goodwyn's house was in front of the new State House at Gervais and Sumter streets.

Since Goodwyn had personal assurances from Sherman that his house would not be burned, he believed that his house and the city would be safe. In his memoirs, Sherman said, "It is probable I told him then not to be uneasy, that we did not intend to stay long, and had no purpose to injure the private citizens or private property."[329]

Mayor T.J. Goodwyn selected the home of Blanton Duncan on Gervais Street as Sherman's headquarters on the site of today's Clarion Town House Hotel. Adapted from an 1872 map of Columbia Source: Library of Congress

Before settling in at the Duncan house, Sherman walked around town. "Before our headquarters-wagons had got up," Sherman said, "I strolled through the streets of Columbia, found sentinels posted at the principal intersections, and generally good order prevailing, but did not again return to the main street, because it was filled with a crowd of citizens watching the soldiers marching by," Sherman said.[330] He had described the fires burning near the City Hall and jail as he came into town, but made no mention of any fire burning at any time that afternoon as he strolled leisurely through the streets, nor did any of his generals.

The Reverend Shand said that the mid-day fires set by Federals in downtown Columbia were out by 2 p.m.[331]

Simms agreed that Sherman and his officers were everywhere on foot, yet, Simms said, they beheld nothing that required the

Federal prisoners had been kept at Camp Sorghum on the west bank of the Congaree near the bridge. They were moved in October 1864 to the grounds of the Asylum (State Hospital) behind the Robert Mills building. This is the way the prison pen at Camp Asylum looked when Sherman arrived in Columbia Courtesy of the South Carolinana Library at the University of South Carolina, Columbia, S.C.

interposition of authority. "And yet robbery was going on at every corner—in nearly every house," Simms said.[332]

Eyewitnesses, including Simms, Goodwyn and Emma LeConte, the 17-year-old daughter of Dr. Joseph LeConte, said looting and pillaging continued all day, but the reign of terror and the fires did not fairly begin until nightfall. "In some instances, where parties complained of the misrule and robbery, their guards said to them, with a chuckle: 'This is nothing. Wait till tonight, and you'll see h.ll.'"[333]

Goodwyn said that Sherman "requested me to call upon him that evening which I did; he appeared very social, spoke kindly and friendly, and promised me most faithfully that our City should be protected, and as safe as if it was in my own hands."[334]

Sherman settled into Duncan's house on Gervais Street in mid-afternoon on February 17.[335] Duncan was a resident of Louisville, Kentucky, and had the contract for manufacturing Confederate money, but he had fled with Hampton's cavalry. The house, which became Sherman's headquarters, was completely furnished with stables and a large yard.

A monument marks the spot where Hampton's Diamond Hill plantation was located at Westminster Street and Stratford Road off Gervais Street. Federals burned his plantation in the late afternoon on Friday, February 17.
Photo by Pat McNeely

As Sherman settled in, he found a paper that had been handed to him by one of the 60 prisoners who had escaped from Camp Asylum. "It proved to be the song of 'Sherman's March to the Sea,' which had been composed by Adjutant S.H.M. Byers, of the Fifth Iowa Infantry, when a prisoner in the asylum at Columbia, which had been beautifully written off by a fellow-prisoner and handed to me in person," Sherman wrote. He liked it so much that he sent for Byers, attached him to his staff, provided him with horse and equipment, and took him as far as Fayetteville, North Carolina, from which Byers was sent to Washington as a bearer of dispatches. Byers later became U.S. consul at Zurich, Switzerland. Byers told Sherman there was an excellent glee-club among the prisoners at Camp Asylum who used to sing it well, "with an audience of rebel ladies," he said. It would be from that song that the title of Sherman's campaign through Georgia would take its name.[336]

"Toward evening of (Friday) February 17th, the mayor, Dr. Goodwin (Goodwyn), came to my quarters at Duncan's house," Sherman said, and the two of them walked together to the home of a member of the Poyas family, who had been his social friends when he was stationed at Fort Moultrie in the 1840s. Their stroll took them from Gervais Street north toward the Charlotte Railroad Depot (near modern Benedict College). There was no sign of smoke or fire in downtown Columbia or the mayor would have been pleading for help and rushing to the scene.

The Poyas' frame house with a high porch was located beyond the Charlotte depot, which was situated in the block bounded by Laurens, Blanding, Barnwell and Richland streets. Sherman "noticed ducks and chickens, and a general air of peace and comfort that was really pleasant to behold at that time of universal desolation." Miss Poyas told Sherman that Yankees had invaded her home soon after Hampton's cavalry had left the city and began looting inside and chasing her chickens and ducks in the yard. When she had showed them a book inscribed by Sherman, the officer called to the others and said, "Boys, that's so; that's Uncle Billy's writing, for I have seen it often before," and he commanded the party to stop pillaging and left a man in charge of the house to protect her. The soldier left to protect her house was apparently one of the few who actually stayed on duty and protected the house after the fires started that night because her house was not listed in Simms inventory of buildings that were burned.[337]

Sherman expressed no surprise or displeasure with his troops who had poured over her fence, chased the chickens and ducks, and even entered the Poyas house, which was against orders. Instead he praised Miss Poyas for her quick wit in saving her home. "Now, this lady had good sense and tact," Sherman said, "and had thus turned aside a party who, in five minutes more, would have rifled her premises of all that was good to eat or wear. I made her a long social visit, and, before leaving Columbia, gave her a half-tierce of rice and about one hundred pounds of ham from our own mess-stores."[338]

As Sherman and Goodwyn parted, Goodwyn said, "He called to me and asked if my water works and fire engines were in good order; in replying, they were; he said that he would be compelled to burn some of our public buildings, but in doing so, he wished to be particular in not injuring any private property; the evening was too windy to proceed now but he would the first calm day."[339] The question was doubly ironic since Sherman would order his troops to destroy the waterworks the next day.

After the visit, Sherman returned to his headquarters. "Having walked over much of the suburbs of Columbia in the afternoon, and being tired, I lay down on a bed in Blanton Duncan's house to rest," Sherman wrote.[340]

Howard had also settled into his headquarters in the Louisa McCord House on Pendleton Street beside South Carolina College, and Logan settled into the Hampton-Preston House at 1616 Blanding Street. General Charles Woods' headquarters were on the southeast corner of Senate and Barnwell streets, which became the site of "Southern Cross," Hampton's last home. Grateful citizens bought the new house for Hampton in 1899.[341]

However, soon after visiting with Sherman, the mayor saw fires starting in the outlying areas. "Gen Hampton's house with the neighboring houses were burnt about sundown in the hours after he bid me good bye and left our section," Goodwyn said. Hampton's home, known as Diamond Hill, was burned. The house was on a site marked by a monument at Westminster Street and Stratford Road off Gervais Street, about 1½ miles from Sherman's headquarters.[342]

Also destroyed was the nearby home of CSA Secretary of the Treasury George A. Trenholm that was located in the general vicinity of Gladden Street off Trenholm Road. Several residents in the area believe his home was called "Fairview" and was at the highest part of Gladden Street, but no historical record seems to exist that shows the exact location.[343]

Also, destroyed that afternoon was Millwood, the best-known of the Hampton plantation homes, which was located about four miles outside of Columbia on Garner's Ferry Road. Hampton's sisters were living there when the home and its extensive library was burned to the ground, leaving only the columns and ruins still visible today on private property still owned by Hampton descendants. A mercury goblet that was stolen from Millwood was returned by the thief after the war and is on display at the South Carolina Confederate Relic Room and Military Museum. Federals also burned Woodlands on the Hampton plantation, the ancestral home that had belonged to Hampton's grandfather.

Hampton's Millwood plantation on Garners Ferry Road was robbed and burned. Only the ruins are left on private property still held by the Hampton family. Source: Library of Congress

Sherman's men destroyed the "beautiful country seats" of Dr. John Wallace, Captain James U. Adams, Mrs. Thomas Stark, Colonel Thomas Taylor (up above Arsenal Hill and behind today's Governor's Mansion), Captain James U. Adams, Mr. Latta, Mrs. English, Mr. C.P. Pelham (Mill Creek) as well as Homestead and many others, according to Simms.[344] "All were robbed and ruined then given to the flames and from these places were carried off all horses mules cattle hogs and stock of every sort and the provisions not carried off were destroyed," Simms said.[345] The billowing smoke from the fires was clearly visible from Simms' office at Washington and Main streets. His office was just two blocks away from Goodwyn's house in front of the State House and within a few blocks of the downtown headquarters of Sherman and his generals.

William H. Orchard, who lived on Taylor (or Camden) Street between Marion and Sumter streets, said he was visited about 7 p.m. by a squad of six or seven soldiers who were guarding the area. As they were leaving, one of the soldiers called to him and said he wished to speak to him alone. "He then said to me in an undertone," Orchard said, "'you seem to be a clever sort of a man, and have a large family, so I will give you some advice: If you have anything you wish to save, take care of it at once, for before morning this d__d town will be in ashes—every house in it.' My only reply was: can that be true? He said, 'yes, and if you do not believe me you will be the sufferer; if you watch you will see three rockets go up soon, and if you do not take my advice you will see h-ll.'"[346]

It was almost dark when Goodwyn returned from his walk with Sherman to find the same "good Christian soldier" who had been there all day as guard and protection to his family. The guard "remained until dark when three rockets went up (of different colors); the soldier then got up and said: I was in hopes the sacking of the City would be sufficient revenge. The guard said that it was possibly coming to the worst. My wife asked him what it meant. He made no reply but left immediately," Goodwyn said, and in less than 20 minutes, he was alarmed to see a fire break out on Main Street near his house.[347] At various parts of the town, Sherman's soldiers had told numerous other citizens that the rockets were the appointed signal for a general conflagration.[348]

A strong wind was blowing from the west that night, and Simms reported that the first fires of the evening broke out west of Main and Sumter streets in some low wooden houses on Gervais Street—mostly brothels. Almost at the same time, a "gang of banditti, sent forth to forage—foraging in Gen. Sherman's dictionary, being identical with burglary and arson," had scattered east of the city, robbing, pillaging and burning, Simms said.[349]

Only a few minutes elapsed before fires in quick succession broke out all around the city and at intervals from each other so distant that they could not have spread to the others, according to Simms.[350]

As fires flared up in various quarters of the city on the signal of the three rockets, "The citizens brought out the fire engines and hose, but the soldiers prevented them from using these by disabling the engines and cutting the hose with their sabres," Simms said. "As the fire made headway, the troops became madder and madder. A perfect carnival of pillage ensued."[351] Goodwyn had hurried to the fire on Richardson (Main) Street. "I went there (was my duty) and struggled hard to suppress it, but our hoses were cut and I found it useless," he said. "On my return home I discovered the City on fire in a great many places. I then tried to save some of my property but the soldiers mocked me and took away everything that I tried to save."[352]

Gibbes, too, saw rockets ascend. "Shortly after this my store, which was on Main street, a few doors south of the market, was set on fire, and immediately after this I saw fires arising in various parts of the city, and in a very short time nearly the whole of Richardson or Main street was in flames."[353]

Gibbes saw several instances of Federal soldiers actually applying fire to buildings and others carrying torches in various part of the city for the same purpose. "I conversed freely with the soldiers of Gen. Sherman's army, both at the time of the burning and afterwards, and no one ever denied the act, but several expressed regret that the entire city was not destroyed," he said. "I saw numbers of them at the scene of the burning, giving expressions and demonstrations of satisfaction by dancing and otherwise. Every house from one square south of the State house to Upper Boundary (Elmwood street) on Main street, which includes all the business

The statue of General Wade Hampton faces north on the grounds of the new State House that survived the burning of Columbia. *Photo by Pat McNeely*

houses, were burnt up, excepting one small house in the extreme northern portion of Main street. All the storehouses containing cotton were burned; and my observation was, that every bale of cotton in Columbia at that time was burned. The large warehouses in the northern portion of Main street were all burned."[354]

When Howard was asked if he had been ordered to destroy any private property except cotton on the march from Savannah to Goldsboro, he said, "I do not remember any.... I think I can state positively that there was nothing else, purely private, except...one pile of corn, ordered to be destroyed."[1]

LeConte said a number of officers had hinted before he left town about certain rockets that would signal the destruction of the city. Although he was about 20 miles away when the city burned, his family told him about the signal rockets that went up from various parts of the city at dark and "instantly fires burst out everywhere," he said.

"In an hour Columbia was a roaring, surging sea of flames. The streets were filled with ten thousand yelling soldiers, running from house to house with flaming torches, and even stealing their trinkets from the frightened women who rushed into the streets from their burning homes. Every house in the city, except those within the campus walls, was pillaged, and most of them first pillaged and then burned. Since the College buildings were used as a hospital for soldiers of both sides, a guard was placed around them to protect them, but in spite of this they were several times fired and saved only by the exertions of the physicians."[355]

When asked during hearings after the war about the rockets that were supposed to have signaled the beginning of the burning of Columbia, Howard said that it was customary for the signal officers to communicate by flags in the daytime and by rockets at night.

"The signals (that night) meant nothing else that I know of," Howard said, and he denied having seen the rockets on the night of February 17.[356]

After the fires began that evening, Goodwyn gave up in "despair" and returned with his wife to the College green (the USC Horseshoe); "Whilst there many good Christian soldiers would come and converse with me, and appear to regret very much our situation," he said. "I asked them at different times if they thought it was an accident, and they invariably replied, No, that from the first night they left Savannah, Georgia until they arrived in Columbia, it was a camp talk what they would do with our City."[357]

When asked about any understanding that Columbia was to be destroyed, Howard said, "By the officers there was a distinct understanding that it should not be destroyed, and those were the orders; that is, the private property, asylums, &c.; on the part of the men, I don't know anything about it." He added that there might have been a plot on the part of the Federal prisoners, who had been released from the jail.

Yet, Howard was visited at his headquarters in Charleston in November of 1865 by the Reverend Shand, who said, "General Howard expressed his regret at the occurrence, and added the following words: 'Though General Sherman did not order the burning of the town, yet somehow or other, the men had taken up the idea that, if they destroyed the capital of South Carolina, it would be peculiarly gratifying to General Sherman.' These were his words, in the order in which I have set them forth.

"I noted them down as having great significancy, and they are as fresh in my remembrance as they were immediately after they

Governor James L. Orr
Courtesy: Library of Congress

were spoken. My friend (whose recollection accords fully with my own) and myself, on our way home, talked the matter over, and could not but be struck...by the fact that although General Howard said that General Sherman did not order the burning, he did not state that General Sherman gave orders that the city should not be burned."[358]

Gibbes was present in the office of Governor James Orr sometime in 1867 when Howard was visiting Columbia.

"Seeing Gen. Hampton across the street, I hailed him from the window, and when he entered Governor Orr introduced him to Gen. Howard. The first thing Gen. Hampton said was: 'Gen. Howard, who burned Columbia?' Gen. Howard laughed and said: 'Why, General, of course we did.' But afterward qualified it by saying: 'Do not understand me to say that it was done by orders.'"[359]

11 THE FATE OF COLUMBIA IS SETTLED

A friend who sought to extinguish the fire kindled in his parlor,
was seized by the collar and hurled aside, with the ejaculation,
'Let the d-----d house burn.'

—*James G. Gibbes*

Colonel Charles Stone, Howard's aide who had accepted the surrender of Columbia earlier that morning, witnessed the first fires break out in the evening. "The wind after sunset had increased in violence, and about 9 o'clock was blowing almost a hurricane from Colonel Palmer's district right towards the heart of the city," according to Stone. "Almost at once, 15 or 20 different flames, from as many different places along the river, shot up, and in ten minutes the fate of Columbia was settled."[360]

Simms, too, said, "There were then some twenty fires in full blast, in as many different quarters, and while the alarm sounded from these quarters, a similar alarm was sent up almost simultaneously from Cotton Town, the Northernmost limit of the city, and from Main street in its very centre, at the several stores or houses of O. Z. Bates, C. D. Eberhardt, and some others, in the heart of the most densely settled portion of the town; thus enveloping in flames almost every section of the devoted city." [361]

As the fires spread through Columbia, the streets were filled with terror-stricken women and children carrying their clothes and valuables tied in sheets. "The bundles in numerous instances were snatched away from them by the soldiers, great numbers of whom were by that time crazed by liquors, pillaged from the cellars of the city," Simms said.[362]

U.S. Captain W. B. Stanley testified that several times during the night he saw Sherman's soldiers take from women bundles of clothes and provisions, open them, take what they wanted and throw the rest into the flames. "Men were violently seized and threatened with the halter or the pistole (sic) to compel them to disclose where their gold or silver was hidden," he said.[363]

The Hanoverian consul, who was in Columbia that night, said he heard "cries of distress from women and children pursued by the

Patricia G. McNeely

The Ursuline Convent located at Blanding and Richardson (Main) streets (where Tapp's is today) was pillaged and torched by Federal troops. Sister Baptista Lynch, the Mother Superior, led her students across Main to St. Peter's Catholic Church on Assembly, but the soldiers followed them and started trying to set fire to St. Peter's. Two Irish Catholic Federal guards stayed on duty and saved St. Peter's, but the Mother Superior led her charges into the graveyard where they spent the night. Courtesy of the South Caroliniana Library at the University of South Carolina, Columbia, S.C.

Federal soldiers, saw rings snatched from the women's fingers by the soldiers, earrings pulled out of their ears, and their clothing torn off."[364] Numerous homeless Columbians made their way to the Asylum grounds and spent the night under the trees and in Camp Asylum where the Federal prisoners-of-war had been held.[365]

After walking around the town for a couple of hours that afternoon, Sherman had relaxed in his room until nightfall. "Soon after dark I became conscious that a bright light was shining on the walls; and, calling some one of my staff (Major Nichols, I think) to inquire the cause, he said there seemed to be a house on fire down about the market-house," Sherman wrote.[366]

"The same high wind prevailed, and, fearing the consequences, I bade him go in person to see if the provost-guard were doing its duty. He soon returned, and reported that the block of buildings directly opposite the burning cotton of that morning was on fire, and that it was spreading, but he had found General Woods in the group with plenty of men trying to put the fire out, or, at least to prevent its extension. The fire continued to increase, and the whole heavens became lurid."[367]

Still, Sherman stayed in his quarters four blocks east of the State House on Gervais Street sending "messenger after messenger to Generals Howard, Logan, and Woods, and received from them repeated assurances that all was being done that could be done, but that the high wind was spreading the flames beyond all control."[368]

In spite of the fact that Main Street was almost entirely engulfed in flames, Sherman did not walk downtown until about 11 p.m., when he could see the "flames rising high in the air, and could hear the roaring of the fire."[369] In spite of the burning and torching going on both inside and outside private homes and

The Hampton-Preston House survived because the Mother Superior from the Ursuline Convent selected it after her building was destroyed by Sherman's soldiers. Federal General John Logan was angry and sorely disappointed because he had prepped the building to be burned as he departed. Photo by Pat McNeely

churches, Sherman said, "The men seemed generally under good control, and certainly labored hard to girdle the fire to prevent its spreading; but, so long as the high wind prevailed, it was simply beyond human possibility."[370]

The men who were "generally under good control" were at that moment pillaging and torching the Ursuline Convent at Main and Blanding streets (where Tapp's is today). Sister Baptista Lynch, the Mother Superior of the convent and academy, had been visited early that morning by a Federal major, who had described himself as an editor from Detroit.[371] Sherman's daughter Minnie had once been a student of the Mother Superior in Brown County, Ohio,[372] and the major had spoken with assurance about saving the convent when he left to ask Sherman for guards. When he returned with eight or ten men, she was encouraged until he leaned over as he was leaving and whispered: "For I must tell you, my sister, that Columbia is a doomed city!" The guards he left behind became the busiest plunderers, Simms said.[373]

As predicted by the Federal major, the convent was set on fire by soldiers late that evening, and the Mother Superior and the Sisters made their way out of the burning building down the street to St. Peter's Catholic Church on the west side of Assembly Street. The sisters retired inside the church that night on slips of bedding, quilts and coverlets, but Sherman's soldiers followed them and began trying to set fire to St. Peter's. Two of Sherman's Irish Catholic guards blocked their efforts, but the worried Mother Superior and her flock spent the night among the gravestones in the church cemetery.[374]

When General Sherman came by the next morning, he expressed his regret at the burning of their convent, "disclaimed the act, attributing it to the intoxication of his soldiers, and told me to choose any house in town for a convent, and it should be ours, " the Mother Superior said. He delegated Colonel Charles Ewing to assist in her selection, so she asked Ewing for "General Preston's house (the Hampton-Preston House), which is large. 'That is where General Logan holds his headquarters,' said he, 'and orders have already been given, I know, to burn it tomorrow morning; but, if you say you will take it for a convent I will speak to the General and the order will be countermanded.'[375]

"On the following morning, after many inquiries, we learned from the officer in charge (General Perry,[376] I think) that his orders were to fire it, unless the Sisters were in actual possession of it, but, if even a 'detachment of Sisters' were in it, it should be spared on their account. Accordingly, we took possession of it, although fires were already kindled near, and the servants were carrying off the bedding and furniture, in view of the house being consigned to the flames."[377]

Although the Mother Superior had told Sherman that the property was not his to give, she learned afterward that Sherman had actually executed titles to the property and had them sent to her. She later returned the property to General John Preston.[378]

One of the most extensive losses of the evening was the home of Dr.

Dr. Robert W. Gibbes
Courtesy of Gibbes' great-great granddaughter Carolyn White Gibbes.

Robert W. Gibbes, whose three-story fireproof house at Sumter and Plain (Hampton) contained one of the finest collections of art and books in the country. Gibbes was the Confederate Surgeon General of South Carolina and president of the Press Association of the Confederate States of America. Gibbes' son, James, witnessed the destruction of his father's house.

"About seven o'clock in the evening three or four rockets were thrown up in the extreme northwestern portion of the town; immediately after that fire was seen in three different points in the

The home of Dr. Robert W. Gibbes contained some of the finest collections of art and books and artifacts in the country. The house, which was fireproof, was on Plain (Hampton) Street across from the First Baptist Church. The Gibbes house would have survived, but witnesses saw Sherman's soldiers enter the house and set fire to the draperies and furnishings. If you look closely, you can see a man who is believed to be Dr. Gibbes standing at the bottom of his steps. Courtesy of the South Caroliniana Library at the University of South Carolina, Columbia, S.C.

northeastern part of the city," he said. He testified that he saw various soldiers with bottles, with some inflammable materials that he supposed to be turpentine, with which they made fireballs.

Dr. Gibbes' home was a fire-proof brick building that had escaped the flames and was still standing at midnight on Friday, February 17. The house would have survived if 15 to 20 soldiers had not entered the home at 2 a.m. on Saturday, February 18 and torched the interior. The younger Gibbes saw Federal soldiers fire the furniture in his father's house, turn over the piano, tables, chairs and start the fire from lace curtains that they lit from the gas lights. He said there was a crowd present at his father's house, who did their best to stop these proceedings, but were powerless.[379]

Gibbes' home contained nearly 200 paintings of enormous value, including originals and copies by European hands and the best engravings from "the most famous pictures of the old masters and by the most excellent engravers of the age." His library was a rich collection of American and South Carolina history, and his cabinet of Southern fossils and memorials contained at least 10,000 specimens. His collection of sharks' teeth was pronounced by Agassiz to be the "finest in the world."

Dr. Gibbes' house (21) on Plain (Hampton) was burned. It was across from the First Baptist Church (20), which survived. The Washington Street Methodist Church (17) was burned but the First Presbyterian Church (15) survived. The offices of the Daily South Carolinian (12) on Washington Street were burned. The new State House (1) survived, but the old State House (2) at the corner of Assembly and Gervais was burned. Trinity Episcopal Church (3) was saved. The City Hall (11) and the courthouse (13) were both destroyed. Adapted from an 1872 map: Source: Library of Congress

His magnificent collections of historical documents and original correspondence of the Revolution, especially South Carolina, were large and valuable. From these, he had compiled and edited three volumes and was in the process of transferring his material to the Historical Society of South Carolina. He also lost a collection of autographs of eminent correspondents in every department of letters, science and art, as well as relics from the pyramids and tombs of Egypt, Pompeii and Mexico, with numerous memorials from the Revolutionary and recent battlefields of the country, pictures from Washington Allston, Sully, Inman, Charles Fraser and DeVeaux, and many originals and copies.[380]

Gibbes said the men who fired his father's house in his presence were sober. "A friend who sought to extinguish the fire kindled in his parlor, was seized by the collar and hurled aside, with the ejaculation, 'Let the d-----d house burn.'"[381]

Days later, Dr. Gibbes discovered that one of the few items that he was able to save that night was the

Dr. Gibbes saved his silver and gold goblet by hiding it under the steps of his house, which was burned by Sherman's troops. Photo by Pat McNeely Courtesy of Gibbes' great-great granddaughter Carolyn Gibbes White

silver and gold goblet that he had hidden under the steps. Gibbes had won $25 and six-and-a-quarter cents in a settlement in a lawsuit against the city of Columbia in 1857 after the Know Nothing government threw him out of a council meeting.[382] The goblet is still owned by Gibbes' direct descendants living in Columbia.[383]

"There were then some twenty fires in full blast, in as many different quarters," according to William Gilmore Simms. "While the alarm sounded from these quarters, a similar alarm was sent up almost simultaneously from Cotton Town, the Northernmost limit of the city, and from Main street in its very centre, at the several stores or houses of O. Z. Bates, C. D. Eberhardt, and some others, in the heart of the most densely settled portion of the town; thus enveloping in flames almost every section of the devoted city."
Source: Library of Congress

Gibbes and his father also lost a uniform manufacturing plant located on Richardson (Main) Street that used the cloth from Columbia (or Saluda) Mills, which they had owned until they sold it in 1862.[384] They were manufacturing Confederate uniforms at their plant, which took up the entire eastern side of the block of Richardson (Main) Street between Washington and Plain (Hampton) streets. There about 35 tailors and upwards of 2,000 women who cut and hand-sewed nearly 50,000 uniforms that sold for $25 to $75 each. Cloth, when it could be obtained by Columbians, sold at upwards of $40 for a single yard.[385]

Gibbes' own home escaped the fire, and more than 150 women and children collected at his house during the night of the fire. He also

South Carolina College (University of South Carolina) and Longstreet Theater (4) were used as hospital facilities for both Confederate and Federal soldiers. Except for the president's house at the apex of the Horseshoe, the buildings are the same today. Dr. John LeConte's home (1) was moved away from the corner of Sumter and Pendleton Streets to become Flinn Hall. Caroliniana Library (2) is the oldest free-standing library in the country. Lieber College (3) was the home of Dr. Joseph LeConte, whose daughter Emma wrote a diary about the burning of Columbia. The Louisa McCord House (5) was Howard's headquarters. Trinity Episcopal Church (Cathedral) (6) survived but the parsonage (7) was destroyed. Adapted from an 1872 map Source: Library of Congress

owned another rental house on the south side of Plain (Hampton) Street between Marion and Sumter that was occupied by Dr. Boozer, who was the physician at the penitentiary.

Mrs. Boozer told Gibbes that a Federal soldier, for whom she had performed some kindness, had told her to remove and conceal everything of value; that the town would be destroyed that night. "She came to me and carried me to her house to see these men, who repeated in my presence these statements, but I could not believe it, and dissuaded her from any attempt to remove; I could not believe such a thing possible, but it turned out as they predicted," and Gibbes' rental house was burned to the ground that night.[386]

12 'We'll burn the very stones of South Carolina.'

"'Your gold, silver, watch, jewels,' They gave no time, allowed no pause or hesitation. It was in vain that the woman offered her keys, or proceeded to pen drawer, or wardrobe, or cabinet, or trunk. It was dashed to pieces by axe or gun butt, with the cry, 'We have a shorter way than that!'"
— **William Gilmore Simms**

John A. Civil saw the first fires of the evening start at about seven or eight o'clock on Friday evening, February 17. "At the time I saw the United States soldiers setting fire to houses, the officers present were not assisting them in doing so. I saw one officer attempting to put the fire out. He was the only officer out of them all that I saw attempt to do anything to stop the fire. The officers, when applied to by the members of my family, said they could afford no relief."[387]

As the fires began, both Goodwyn and Simms said they didn't see many drunken soldiers early in the evening and not until a late hour in the night after all the grocery stores on Main Street had been rifled.

"The men engaged did not need the torch," Simms said. "They carried with them, from house to house, pots and vessels containing combustible liquids, composed probably of phosphorous and other similar agents, turpentine, &c.; and with balls of cotton saturated in this liquid with which they also overspread floors and walls, they conveyed the flames with wonderful rapidity from dwelling to dwelling. Each had his ready box of Lucifer matches, and, with a scrape upon the walls, the flames began to rage. Where houses were closely contiguous, a brand from one was the means of conveying destruction to the other."[388]

After leaving his house at about 1 a.m. Saturday morning, Simms saw a party of Federal soldiers break into the residence of C. P. Pelham on the corner of Washington and Bull streets.

"I went to the door and saw these soldiers in the upper part of the building, and in a few minutes afterward I saw the flames break out of the upper part of the building, and it was soon burned down," Simms said. "I saw no other fired by soldiers during the night."[389]

Even though high winds prevailed, the dirt streets were 100 feet wide in most places except for Assembly and Gervais and four other streets, which were 150 feet wide. They had been designed to prevent the spread of fire and disease. Many of the buildings that burned were brick or stone. Some buildings, like the home of Dr. Gibbes, were fireproof and would not have burned without being set on fire from the inside.

Engines and hose were brought out by the firemen, but they were soon driven away by the "pertinacious hostility of the soldiers; the hose was hewn to pieces, and the firemen, dreading worse usage to themselves, left the field in despair," Simms said.[390] The flames continued to spread from "side to side, from front to rear, from street to street by the application of fresh combustibles until by

By midnight on Friday, February 17, all of Richardson (Main) Street from the area north of Upper Boundary (Elmwood Avenue) to the new State House (in distance) was in flames. Sherman's soldiers drank and danced with lighted torches in front of the City Hall at the corner of Richardson (Main) and Washington streets. Source: Library of Congress

midnight, Main street, from its Northern to its Southern extremity, was a solid wall of fire that had consumed by 1 a.m. the banks and Treasury buildings, the Janney's (Congaree) and Nickerson's Hotels, every large block in the business portion of the city; the old Capitol and all adjacent buildings were in ruins," Simms said.[391]

At 1 a.m. on Saturday, February 18, the hour was struck by the clock of the Market Hall, "which was even then illuminated from within," Simms said. "It was its own last hour which it sounded, and its tongue was silenced forevermore. In less than five minutes after, its spire went down with a crash, and, by this time, almost all the buildings within the precinct were a mass of ruins."[392]

The Rev. Lawrence P. O'Connell was the only clergyman in St. Mary's College, a large brick building built in 1852 at the corner of Richardson (Main) and Lumber (Calhoun) streets. St. Mary's was large enough to accommodate more than 100 students and contained a large library and collections of paintings and other treasures. He said he was imprisoned by Sherman's troops and denied the right to even save the holy oils while the soldiers hauled away magnificent paintings, manuscripts of rare value and statuary and drank whiskey from the sacred chalice before setting torches to the building, which burned to the ground that night.[393]

"Ladies were hustled from their chambers—their ornaments plucked from their persons, their bundles from their hands," Simms said. "Men and women bearing off their trunks were seized, despoiled, in a moment the trunk burst asunder with the stroke of axe or gun-butt, the contents laid bare, rifled of all the objects of desire, and the residue sacrificed to the fire. You might see the ruined owner, standing woe-begone, aghast, gazing at his tumbling dwelling, his scattered property, with a dumb agony in his face that was inexpressibly touching. Others you might hear, as we did, with wild blasphemies assailing the justice of Heaven, or invoking, with lifted and clenched hands, the fiery wrath of the avenger. But the soldiers plundered and drank, the fiery work raged, and the moon sailed serenely" over the blazing city.[394]

Within the houses, scenes were even harsher. "'Your gold, silver, watch, jewels.' They gave no time, allowed no pause or hesitation. It was in vain that the woman offered her keys, or proceeded to pen drawer, or wardrobe, or cabinet, or trunk. It was dashed to pieces by axe or gun butt, with the cry, 'We have a shorter way than that!'"[395]

Christ Episcopal Church at the southeast corner of Blanding and Marion streets was one of seven churches burned by the Federals that night. Source: Library of Congress

Nor were these acts those of common soldiers, Simms said. "Commissioned officers, of rank so high as that of a colonel, were frequently among the most active in spoilation, and not always the most tender or considerate in the manner and acting of their crimes."[396]

Through the night, residents fled to churches, but soldiers began burning the churches. Christ Episcopal Church (where the Good Shepherd Episcopal Church at 1512 Blanding Street is today) was destroyed during the night as was Ebenezer Lutheran Church at the corner of Richland and Sumter Streets.[397]

Even though seven churches were burned, the First Baptist Church, where the Secession convention had first met on December 17, 1860, was spared.[398]The local story is that Sherman's soldiers with torches asked a man standing in front of the present-day Baptist

Washington Street Methodist Church at Bull and Marion streets was destroyed by Sherman's troops. Local legend is that the soldiers mistakenly burned the Methodist church because they thought it was the First Baptist Church. Courtesy of the South Caroliniana Library at the University of South Carolina, Columbia, S.C.

Church on Plain (Hampton) Street for directions toward the church.

The man pointed away from the present-day Baptist church that was built in 1859[399] and toward the original site of the First Baptist Church, which was built in 1811 on the Sumter Street corner, where the Washington Street Methodist Church was located.[400] Whether the story is true or not, the soldiers passed by today's First Baptist Church and burned the Methodist church.

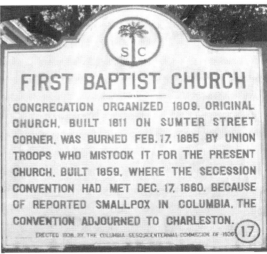

The marker describes the night Sherman's soldiers mistakenly burned another church (the Methodist Church) because they thought it was today's First Baptist Church built in 1859. Photo by Pat McNeely

The destruction of the Methodist church was witnessed by Malcolm Shelton, who lived across the street on the south side of Washington between Bull and Marion streets. Shelton watched with horror as the drama unfolded. He said soldiers with flammable materials set fire to his house twice, but he managed to put out the fires; however, on the third try his house and neighboring dwellings were destroyed.

The Methodist church was located across the street. "I saw the soldiers break in the door of the Washington Street Methodist Church, immediately opposite my own residence, and in a few moments after I saw the smoke and flames coming out of the doors and windows, and the Church was soon consumed. I was in the company of two United States officers at the time of this occurrence, and they with me witnessed it."[401]

Trinity Episcopal Church (Cathedral) survived but the parsonage located south of the new State House was burned.
Acrylic painting by Pat McNeely

The Reverend Shand said, "In my own church (Trinity Episcopal), where a guard had been stationed for its protection, rosin, placed there probably by some of said guard, was found the next day scattered upon the floor, with a view, doubtless, to its conflagration, but, through God's mercy, it escaped the fate intended for it. I could fill many pages with details of circumstances and occurrences conclusive of the fact that the town was fired by the soldiers."[402]

Just before the Trinity parsonage was set on fire, the Reverend Shand tried to save a trunk containing the sacred vessel of his church but it was violently wrested from his keeping. When Sherman reached Camden, he restored what he believed were the vessels to Bishop Davis, but the ministers discovered later that the plate belonged to St. Peter's Church in Charleston.[403] However, Trinity's communion plate was never recovered.[404]

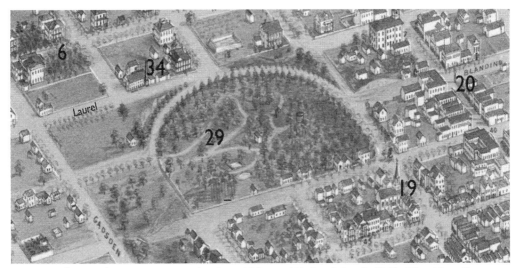

During the night, citizens rushed to Sidney (Finlay) Park (29). The Ursuline convent (20) was burned and the mother superior fled across Assembly Street with her students to St. Peter's Catholic Church (19). The Arsenal Academy (6) was destroyed on Saturday, February 18. The part of it that survived became the governor's mansion. Source: Library of Congress

As the churches were burned, citizens hurried to Sidney (Finlay) Park because there were almost no houses in that neighborhood. However, as soon as they had huddled in the park, "fireballs were thrown from the heights into the deepest hollows of the park, and the wretched fugitives were forced to scatter, finding their way to other places of retreat and finding none of them secure."[405]

Even as the fires were raging through the town, Sherman's soldiers continued their search for loot. "Men could be seen staggering off with huge waiters, vases, candelabra, to say nothing of cups, goblets and smaller vessels, all of solid silver," Simms said.[406] "'And what do you think of the Yankees now?' was a frequent question. 'Do you not fear us, now?' 'What do you think of secession?' &c, &c. 'We mean to wipe you out! We'll burn the very stones of South Carolina.'"[407]

Only a few of the Federal guards obeyed orders to stay at their stations and protect property. The home of Jennie Lee Foard at 1429 Laurel Street was saved, even though nearby homes and Ebenezer Church were destroyed. A guest who was staying with the Foards had known Sherman in Charleston and had visited him on the

Ebenezer Lutheran Church on Richland Street was one of seven churches burned during the night. *Courtesy of the South Caroliniana Library at the University of South Carolina, Columbia, S.C.*

afternoon of February 17 to ask for a guard. The soldier he assigned stayed on duty and saved the Foard house while everything around it burned.[408]

The buildings of the South Carolina College, (now the Horseshoe at the University of South Carolina)[409] including the (South Caroliniana) Library were saved primarily because of the efforts of Professors Maximillian LaBorde, acting president, J. L. Reynolds and W. J. Rivers, and a medical doctor who took their places at the gate of the campus and waited for the Federals to approach. The campus was surrounded by a brick wall that survives today, but instead of two gates as it is today, only a single gate opened into the green.

The mayor, like hundreds of others, fled to the green (the Horseshoe) at South Carolina College where Emma LeConte lived with her family in the (Lieber) Faculty House. By then, all students had enlisted in the Confederate army, but the faculty had stayed on, including Emma's father Dr. Joseph Le Conte,[410] who was a chemistry and geology professor. She was awakened at 4 a.m. on Saturday, February 18, and they all went to the front door.

"My God!—what a scene! It was about four o'clock and the State house was one grand conflagration. Imagine night turned into noonday, only with a blazing, scorching glare that was horrible—a copper colored sky across which swept columns of black rolling smoke glittering with sparks and flying embers, while all around us were falling thickly showers of burning flakes. Everywhere the palpitating blaze walling the streets with solid masses of flames as far as the eye could reach—filling the air with its horrible roar. On every side the crackling and devouring fire, while every instant came the crashing of timbers and the thunder of falling buildings. A quivering molten ocean seemed to fill the air and sky. The (Legislative) Library building opposite us seemed framed by the gushing flames and smoke, while through the windows gleamed the liquid fire."[411]

Their vigil had started around noon on February 17 when the Federals, under the command of a Captain Young, arrived. The professors pleaded for protection for the library and the college buildings, and Young assured them that the college would be spared and left a guard within the walls.

The fires that began early in the night showered sparks on

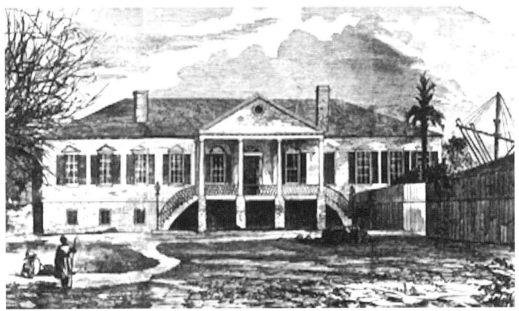

The original State House faced east on Richardson (Main) Street with its back to Assembly. Part of Main Street in front of the old State House was closed to construct the new State House. A monument marks the spot where Sherman's troops set fire to the old State House at about 4 a.m. on Friday, February 18.
Courtesy of the South Caroliniana Library at the University of South Carolina, Columbia, S.C.

houses in the Horseshoe until the roofs of the homes of LaBorde (who lived in the McCutchen House) and Rivers burst into flames, but the fire was contained before the houses burned down. Almost no students had been left on campus after the war started in 1861 and all were gone by 1864 when the college was converted to a soldiers' hospital.[412] With fires raging as close as the Trinity parsonage across the street, patients who could move dragged themselves from their beds and onto the green during the night.[413]Once the destruction of the college seemed so probable that all the patients were moved to the campus green, and the next day more than twenty died because of fright and exposure. At one time, Dr. LeConte's wife thought their home (now Lieber College on the Horseshoe) was doomed, and she spent the greater part of the night with the children around her in the back garden as far from the house as they could get.[414]

Howard's headquarters were in the Louisa McCord house on Pendleton Street diagonally across from Dr. John LeConte's house, which was in later years moved away from the corner and became Flinn Hall. South Caroliniana Library is the first building on the left on the Horseshoe, and Dr. LaBorde lived in the McCutchen House. Dr. Joseph LeConte lived in Lieber College. Longstreet Theatre is at the intersection of Green and Sumter. Adapted from an 1872 map of Columbia. Source: Library of Congress

13 A CITY REDUCED TO ASHES

A square mile of the heart of the city had been eaten out, and the men's appetite for revenge satiated.

—Colonel Charles Stone

Sherman met the Reverend A. Toomer Porter of Charleston in the street between 3 and 4 o'clock Saturday morning, February 18, and "some remark was made...by the General as to the dreadful spectacle before them," Porter said. The scene was most heartrending, "inasmuch as thousands of women and children were deprived of their all, their homes being reduced to ashes, they were compelled on a cold night to congregate together in church yards and open plains."[415]

Porter reported that Sherman lashed out at the drunken condition of his troops and said, "Whoever heard of an evacuated city to be left a depot of liquor for an army to occupy? I found one hundred and twenty casks of whiskey in one cellar. Your Governor, being a lawyer or a judge, refused to have it destroyed, because it was private property, and now my men have got drunk and have got beyond my control and this is the result."[416]

The Reverend A. Toomer Porter of Charleston was present when Sherman issued the order to end the fires. Courtesy of the South Caroliniana Library at the University of South Carolina, Columbia, S.C.

About that time, perceiving an officer on horseback, Sherman said, "Captain Andrews, did I not order that this thing should be stopped?' 'Yes, General,' said the Captain, 'but the first division that came in soon got as drunk as the first regiment that occupied the town.' 'Then, sir,' said General Sherman, 'go and bring in the second division. I hold you personally responsible for its immediate cessation.' The officer darted off and Sherman bade me good evening. I am sure it was not more than an hour and a half from the time that General Sherman gave his order that the city was clear of the destroyers."[417]

Howard had replaced Stone's drunken brigade when he first entered Columbia that morning with a second brigade, who also became drunk. "Finally, I had the whole of one division and a part of another guarding the city, and endeavoring to protect the inhabitants and save all that was possible from the flames," Howard reported, but as numerous civilians reported, most of the guards had abandoned their posts and had joined the wild orgy of arsonists torching the city.[418]

The Reverend Porter witnessed the immediate action caused by Sherman's order. The tap of a drum and the sound of a signal cannon had an immediate effect,[419] and soldiers "supposed to be of Woods' division were seen, having others in charge who had been taken, it was thought, from their incendiary operations and conducting them to the camps outside the city, and in the course of an hour, the flames showed signs of becoming subdued," he said.[420]

Gibbes saw squads of cavalry "galloping through the streets sounding their bugles and calling on the soldiers to fall into ranks."[421] In addition to Woods' two brigades, soldiers from General John M. Oliver's Third Brigade from the 15th Corps poured into the streets, carrying off rioters in groups and squads and extinguishing the fires. The drunken revelry continued for another hour with groups at several corners of the streets, "drinking, roaring, reveling—while the fiddle and accordion were playing their popular airs among them," Simms said.[422]

Most of the rioting soldiers had been hauled away to the camps and the fire was dying down by 5 a.m. when Sherman surveyed the scene and said, "The men seemed generally under good control." By then, two of his soldiers had been killed, 30 had been wounded and more than 3,500 drunk and disorderly Federals and civilians had been arrested.[423]

No one would ever be court-martialed or shot for pillaging and burning Columbia, and Sherman's order to stop the burning had come too late for the old State House. The building had been torched at 4 a.m. along with the Legislative library, which consisted of 25,000 volumes. The destruction of the old State House and other houses up and down Richardson (Main) Street by Sherman's soldiers had been witnessed by residents who had personally seen his men setting fire to the inside of their homes, businesses and churches. The civilians, most with only the clothes on their backs, were seeking shelter and already accusing Sherman's troops of sacking, robbing, pillaging and destroying the city.[424]

"But the danger, even then, was not over," Simms said.[425]

Dr. Maximilian LaBorde was acting president of South Carolina College in 1865 and played a key role in saving the campus. Courtesy of the South Caroliniana Library at the University of South Carolina, Columbia, S.C.

"About 8 a.m., the College gate was assaulted by a band of drunken cavalry, one hundred and fifty or more, bent upon penetrating the campus, and swearing to fire the buildings. The officer in command of the guard reported to the professors that his force was not adequate to the protection of the establishment, and that he was about to be overwhelmed."[426]

Professors LaBorde and Rivers and one of the surgeons ran to the headquarters of Howard, who was staying in the Louisa McCord house on Pendleton Street across from the brick wall of the Horseshoe. They appealed to him to redeem his pledge to protect the College and its library (Caroliniana).

He commanded Stone to "arrest the danger." Stone hurried around the corner to the front of the campus on Sumter Street and with only one revolver in hand succeeded in dispersing the incendiary cavalry.[427] Although many surrounding buildings burned, including the old State House across the street, the original buildings of South Carolina College were saved.

As a result of the fires that raged from dark on Friday, February 17 until early Saturday morning, February 18, Stone said that "a square mile of the heart of the city had been eaten out, and the men's appetite for revenge satiated."[428] From that time until Sherman's departure from Columbia (with perhaps one or two exceptions), not another private dwelling was burned by his soldiers, and during the succeeding days and nights of his occupation, perfect tranquility prevailed throughout the town.[429]

And in spite of Sherman's personal assurances, Goodwyn's house at Gervais and Sumter streets had been burned to the ground during the night of February 17, along with, according to Simms, three-fifths of the city and selected outlying private homes. In a letter to the governor on February 26, Goodwyn insisted that four-fifths of the city lay in ruins. Those who would tell similar stories included dozens of Columbia residents, including Alfred Huger, Ex-Senator and Colonel Arthur P. Hayne, James Rose, Dr. Templeton, and J.K. Robinson.

Mayor Goodwyn said, "Gen. Howard called upon me the next day and said Gen. Sherman would like to see me." It would be Sherman's second attempt to blame the nearest Confederate for the burning of Columbia. "I then called upon the Genl and he said to me that he regretted very much the burning of our beautiful City and that it was my fault in suffering liquor to be left in the City after it was evacuated by our forces. Who could command drunken soldiers."[430]

Even Howard, who Simms said was once a "pious parson," told a citizen complaining about the "monstrous crime of which his army had been guilty: 'It is only what the country deserves. It is her fit punishment; and if this does not quiet rebellion, and we have to return, we will do this work thoroughly. We will not leave woman or child.'"[431]

As Sherman's soldiers plundered and drank into the night, some had fallen into the flames. Numerous Columbians reported that Federal soldiers were burned to death that night "in the luxurious beds of the beautiful homes of Columbia," according to Frank F. Whilden. "They had retired too drunk even to take their boots off, and when the houses went up in flames, they were consumed. One skeleton of a soldier was found in the back part of our house on

Laurel street the morning after the fire, completely cremated, all but the brass buttons and belt buckle."[432]

Although Howard would admit in 1872 that "many of our own soldiers were burnt up that night," he did not report the number.[433] "A large number of our men, who perhaps drank whisky for the first time when it was brought to them that day in buckets, became blindly drunk, and hundreds perished in the flames in spite of all the efforts of their comrades to save them," Howard said.[434]

Sherman never reported the "hundreds" of his drunken men who were burned to death in the fires that they set during the night of February 17. Simms, however, said, "Rye, corn, claret and Madeira all found their way into the same channels, and we are not to wonder, when told that no less than one hundred and fifty of the drunken creatures perished miserably among the flames kindled by their own comrades, and from which they were unable to escape.[435]

"By others, however, the estimate is reduced to thirty; but the number will never be known. Sherman's officers themselves are reported to have said that they lost more men in the sack and burning of the city (including certain explosions) than in all their fights while approaching it. It is also suggested that the orders which Sherman issued at daylight, on Saturday morning, for the arrest of the fire, were issued in consequence of the loss of men which he had thus sustained."[436]

After Sherman's brief moments of blaming first the governor and then the mayor for the fire because of all the liquor in the city, Sherman had to realize that blaming South Carolina officials for having too much liquor in the city was actually blaming his own troops, which he would never do. So, in his third story—the one that would stick—he dropped all accusations about liquor and his men being drunk and blamed the nearest Confederate, who happened to be Hampton camped 20 miles away at Ridgeway. As Sherman settled in on what would be his final account of the burning of Columbia, he would say that "the destruction of property in Columbia had nothing to do with his federal troops" but had been caused by cotton that had been left burning in the street by Hampton.

He would write later: "The whole subject has since been thoroughly and judicially investigated, in some cotton cases, by the

Mixed Commission on American and British claims, which commission failed to award a verdict in favor of the English claimants, and thereby settled the fact that the destruction of property in Columbia, during that night, did not result from the acts of the General Government of the United States—that is to say, from my army."[437]

In his meeting with Sherman after the fire, Goodwyn, who had been Sherman's second nearest Confederate to blame for the burning of Columbia, said, "There were no allusions made to previous fire, to accident, or to Genl Hampton; the fact is Gen Hampton had no more to do with the burning of Columbia that you had; it is his native city and every man that lived in it was his friend and he knew it and would he render them all penniless and houseless; the charge is absurd."[438]

Goodwyn, who had dealt directly with Sherman and walked the streets of Columbia with him during the occupation, was very emphatic about who burned Columbia. "The soldiers of Genl Sherman's Army burnt Columbia," he wrote.[439] In a "nervous and hurried" letter to the governor on February 26, Goodwyn said, "I know Gov that when you heard of our distress that you would from your heart sympathise with us; we have been truly badly & cruelly treated, by a lying and savage foe. They promised perfect protection (Sherman) to all private property & persons—when it can be proved that they contemplated our utter Destruction weeks before they came here."[440]

Goodwyn, whose house was destroyed after his guard abandoned his post, "became completely worn out from fatigue and anxiety when Sherman left us," according to E. J. Scott.[441] Goodwyn soon moved his family to another home 40 miles away at Fort Motte in modern-day Calhoun County, and citizens sent for Gibbes at the State House yard and begged him "to take hold of the government of the city."[442] Gibbes would be mayor through 1866. Goodwyn continued to live at Fort Motte until he found his final resting place after the war in the cemetery at Trinity Cathedral in Columbia.[443]

In a deposition after the war, Hampton said it would be impossible "in an equal number of paragraphs" to express "a greater number of falsehoods" than those expressed by Sherman on the burning of Columbia. "I did not order any cotton 'moved into the street and fired,' he said. "On the contrary, my first act on taking command of the cavalry, to which I was assigned only the night before the evacuation of Columbia, was to represent to Gen. Beauregard, the danger to the town by firing the cotton in the streets. Upon this representation he authorized me to give orders that no cotton in the town should be fire, which order was strictly carried out. I left the city after the head of Sherman's column entered it, and I assert, what can be proved by thousands, that not one bale of cotton was on fire when he took possession of the city. His assertion to the contrary is false, and he knows it to be so. A distinguished citizen of this State, whose name, were I at liberty to give it, would be a sufficient voucher even at the North, for the truth of any statement made by him, has given to the public a minute history of the destruction of the city. From his document, which is too long for insertion in your paper, I make a few extracts which will show how true is Gen. Sherman's solemn disclaimer of 'any agency in this fire' and his claim to have 'saved what of Columbia remains unconsumed.'"[444]

The Reverend Shand said, "I do not believe that (General Sherman) literally ordered the city to be consumed. To have done so would have left him no possible means of evading the accusation of his culpability. That he gave no decided nor positive order, however, that it should not be burned, nor took any steps to prevent its burning, but rather winked and connived at it, is to my mind absolutely certain.[445]

"Although General Sherman may not have given an express order for the burning of the city, he will not, I think, deny that he did extend to his men a license to sack the city and commit other acts of atrocity for a certain number of hours, with the exception, perhaps, of the murder of the citizens and one or two other heinous crimes."

The Reverend Shand, whose parsonage on south Main at Senate behind the new State House had been torched along with Trinity's Sunday School house, had taken shelter with a friend who still had a house. "And I met there a lieutenant of the army, a Christian and humane man, who had been chiefly instrumental in saving the house," the Reverend Shand said. "He seemed filled with horror at the occurrence of the previous night, which he said exceeded anything in point of enormity that he had witnessed on the most sanguinary battle fields, and although he did not admit that General S. had directed the city to be burned; he did not deny that its destruction had been pre-determined. My friends' residence had been in imminent peril, and he had removed his family from it during the night but remained in it himself and at or about the dawn of day, a loud bugle blast was sounded, when the lieutenant said to him, 'You may go and bring your family home. That bugle is the signal for the cessation of the work of destruction, and a very strong police will immediately be sent out to protect and guard the city."[446]

The Reverend Shand even itemized reasons for concluding that Sherman's troops burned the city with his acquiescence. He cited a letter between Halleck and Sherman when Sherman said that Logan's corps that would enter Columbia "never left its work half-done," a corps that the Reverend Shand was told by one of Sherman's own officers was "confessedly composed of the most brutal men in the whole army and was always placed in front when any signal and extraordinary infliction of violence was to be visited upon a people." His second reason was the admirable discipline of Sherman's army. "No soldier of his would have dared to do what, even in minor matters, was known to be displeasing to him, far less to disobey a peremptory order." And third, "a word from General Sherman would have prevented the appalling catastrophe."[447]

Others who were in the city were just as certain about Sherman's responsibility and made similar statements, including Simms, who was co-editor of city's daily newspaper. His office, which was located on Washington between Sumter and Richardson (Main) streets, was destroyed during the night as well.

Another of the eye-witnesses was Dr. Daniel H. Trezevant, whose house across the street from the Baptist Church on Plain (now Hampton) Street, was burned to the ground that night. Trezevant said, "The suburbs were first set on fire"—by whom? the prisoners and soldiers and negroes for it was not within 500 yards of the cotton that Sherman saw burning... Pillaging gangs soon fired the heart of the town, then entered the houses, in many instances, carrying off articles of value. The flames soon burst out in all parts of the town.... I trust I shall never witness such a scene again—drunken soldiers rushing from house to house, emptying them of their valuables, and then firing them."[448]

Trezevant said, "It is important to bear these facts in memory, as it will be seen that when Sherman gives an account of the catastrophe to free himself from blame, he changes the whole order of the affair and makes the fires to have been burning all day, but leaping into life and activity when the night came on, and requiring him to call for additional assistance." Trezevant said that if the Federals worked so hard to save life and property as they claimed, how was it that so many "silver goblets, &c., had found their way into the camp?"[449]

Conyngham reported that soldiers from the 29th Missouri were left to patrol the streets, but, "I did not once see them interfering with the groups that rushed about to fire and pillage the houses.[450] True, Generals Sherman, Howard, and others were out giving instructions for putting out a fire in one place, while a hundred fires were lighting all round them. How much better would it have been had they brought in a division or brigade of sober troops, and cleared out the town, even with steel and bullets!"[451]

Charleston was under siege by Federal forces for 567 days before being evacuated without a fight on Friday February 17, the same night that the people of Columbia saw their city go up in flames. Fort Sumter had been reduced to rubble. Source: Library of Congress

Conyngham wanted to blame everybody for the burning of Columbia. He blamed "inebriated soldiers, escaped prisoners and negroes," but he also said, "Governor McGrath and General Wade Hampton are partly accountable for the destruction of their city. General Beauregard, the major, Mr. Goodwin, and others wanted to send a deputation as far as Orangeburg, which is 40 miles away, to surrender the city, and, when evacuating, to destroy all the liquors. In both of these wise views they were overruled by the governor and Wade Hampton, the latter staying that he would defend the town from house to house. On the other hand I must honestly say that I saw nothing to prevent General Woods, who was in command there, from bringing sufficient troops to clear out the place, or his superior generals either from putting a stop to such disgraceful scenes."[452]

Lamely, Conyngham admitted that Sherman's troops were in such control that they were able to save the houses of the "Prestons, Houystons, and other wealthy secesh occupied as official quarters."

For more than a decade, Sherman stuck to the story about Hampton leaving cotton burning in the streets before he finally admitted in his memoirs in 1875 that he had blamed the nearest Confederate in his continuing effort to undermine and destroy civilian support for Hampton and the Confederate cause. "In my official report of this conflagration, I distinctly charged it to General Wade Hampton, and confess I did so pointedly, to shake the faith of his people in him, for he was in my opinion boastful, and professed to be the special champion of South Carolina."[453]

And on the same night that the people of Columbia were watching their city go up in flames, Charleston was evacuated. U.S. Admiral John A. Dahlgren said he had seen no manifestation of weakness or intention to abandon Charleston until a few hours before the fact, but the main bodies of the Confederate army left during the evening on Friday, February 17 and were gone by the morning of February 18. The streets of Charleston where the war had begun were empty by mid-morning when Dahlgren and a group of naval captains walked through the streets. "All was silent as the grave," he said. "No one to be seen but a few firemen."[454]

14 WHO BURNED COLUMBIA?

I disclaim on the part of my army any agency in this fire, but, on the contrary, claim that we saved what of Columbia remains unconsumed. And without hesitation I charge General Wade Hampton with having burned his own city of Columbia.

—*William T. Sherman*

The morning sun rose bright and clear over the ruined city of Columbia on Saturday, February 18, "About half of it was in ashes and in smouldering heaps," Sherman said. "Many of the people were houseless, and gathered in groups in the suburbs, or in the open parks and spaces, around their scanty piles of furniture."[455]

The business section of the city, the largest churches, and the wealthiest residences lay in ashes, Sherman said, and the fire had "burned out the very heart of the city, embracing several churches, the old State-House, and the school or asylum of that very Sister of Charity who had appealed for my personal protection. Nickerson's

Richardson (Main) Street looking north from the new State House shows the destruction on both sides of the street as it looked on the morning of Saturday, February 18, 1865. *Courtesy of the South Caroliniana Library at the University of South Carolina, Columbia, S.C.*

Hotel, in which several of my staff were quartered, was burned down, but the houses occupied by myself, Generals Howard and Logan, were not burned at all."[456]

City Alderman Bates said he called on an officer of the day at his headquarters on Plain (Hampton) Street on February 18, and was shown the new order issued by Sherman that forbade the firing of any house in the city, either by soldier or citizen, on penalty of being shot. "After that time, the fire occurred at Adam Edgar's and at other places. These fires were extinguished by the aid of the United States soldiers. I do not know of any assistance rendered by the United States soldiers in suppressing the fire on the day and night of the 17th of February."[457]

Sherman had finally issued the order to "not burn" and to "not destroy" private property on penalty of being shot, but destruction of government property was just beginning.

Howard's troops followed the railroad tracks south toward the Wateree and burned the significant railroad town of Kingville in Lower Richland County and destroyed 3,000 feet of track that ran beside it. The town had been established in 1840 as a station on the line from Charleston to Columbia. The Federals destroyed a hotel, post office, shops, offices and private residences.[458]

Local lore is that Wavering Plantation in Lower Richland was spared because the owner had gone to medical school with one of the Federal officers. Sherman's troops passed over Goodwill Plantation on the Garners Ferry Road in Lower Richland County, which had been developed as a rice and cotton plantation in 1795 and was one of the largest rice plantations in the country.[459] Kensington Mansion, which was built in 1854, was also spared.

While soldiers were foraging through Lower Richland county, his troops in Columbia continued to set fires to Confederate arms and ammunition, to factories and munitions piles, to the city gas works and machinery in the railroad yards and the city waterworks in Sidney Park—all burned, blasted, disabled. Another thousand bales of cotton were torched, this time in a controlled fire. Another detail under the supervision of Colonel O. M. Poe destroyed the State Arsenal, where the governor's home is today. Arsenal Academy, which had been the state arsenal, occupied the square bounded by

Richland and Lincoln streets from 1842 to 1865 when Sherman's troops burned all the academy buildings except officers' quarters, which had been built in 1855. The officers' quarters would become the Governor's Mansion in 1868.[460]

While the Federals were hauling shot, shell and ammunition from the Arsenal to dump in the river, some of it hit percussion shells and exploded, killing sixteen men, the only casualties that Sherman reported in Columbia.[461] Federals also destroyed the Palmetto Armory located at the southwest corner of Richland and Lincoln and later called Palmetto Iron works. Although it was originally built to convert flint and steel muskets into percussion guns, arms and munitions were manufactured there from 1861 to 1865.[462]

The Federals also destroyed several valuable foundries and the Confederate Printing Plant (now Publix) on Gervais Street where money had been printed. "The dies had been carried away, but about sixty handpresses remained," Sherman said. "There was also found an

Federals burned all of the buildings of the Arsenal Academy except for the officers' quarters, which became the Governor's Mansion in 1868. Photo by Pat McNeely

immense quantity of money, in various states of manufacture, which our men spent and gambled with in the most lavish manner."[463]

As soon as the fires died down, Simms began a meticulous inventory of the destruction, which he published first in *The Phoenix,* a newspaper that he and Julian Selby started after Sherman left the city.

"It has pleased God, in that Providence which is so inscrutable to man, to visit our beautiful city with the most cruel fate which can ever befall States or cities," Simms wrote. "He has permitted an invading army to penetrate our country almost without impediment; to rob and ravage our dwellings, and to commit three-fifths of our city to the flames. Eighty four squares, out of one hundred and twenty-four (!) which the city contains, have been destroyed, with scarcely the exception of a single house. The ancient capitol building of the State—that venerable structure, which, for seventy years, has echoed with the eloquence and wisdom of the most famous statesmen—is laid in ashes."

Courtesy of the South Caroliniana Library at the University of South Carolina, Columbia, S.C.

Simms said six temples of the Most High God had shared the same fate, along with 11 banks, schools, shops of art and trade, of invention and manufacture; shrines and "shrines equally of religion,

Only the shells of buildings can be seen at the intersection of Laurel and Richardson (Main) streets. Courtesy of the South Caroliniana Library at the University of South Carolina, Columbia, S.C.

benevolence and industry; are all buried together, in one congregated ruin."[464]

Simms' bill of particulars, published with a list of the houses and buildings destroyed on the night of February 17, "was dismissed as self-serving and erroneous by Harper's Illustrated, which had been reporting the war blow-by-blow for a northern audience since Fort Sumter," according to historian Theodore Rosengarten. Taking Sherman at his word, Harper's version of Sherman's account is still being quoted, so that the official federal version of events in Columbia can be found without alteration in works such as Lieutenant Colonel Joseph B. Mitchell's Decisive Battles of the Civil War, and George Fort Milton's Conflict: The American Civil War—"which goes to show that historians may not always read the primary sources, but they always read each other," Rosengarten said.[465]

Simms said that Masonic brethren told others in the city that an order had been issued to the troops before they crossed the river, giving them license to sack, plunder and destroy for the space of thirty-six hours, and that Columbia was destined for destruction. A sick Federal soldier, who had been fed, nursed and kindly treated by a city lady, told her on Friday morning (February 17) that the place would be destroyed that night.

"The simultaneous breaking out of the fires, in the heart of the city, and in the suburbs in twenty places besides, should conclude all doubt."[466]

The offices of the *Daily South Carolinian* newspaper on Washington between Main and Sumter were near the spot where the fires had started in the middle of the day, but the newspaper office was not destroyed until late that evening. When Simms learned the next day that Sherman was accusing Hampton of starting the fire, Simms was outraged that anyone would believe that Sherman's troops had not burned the city. "If it could be shown that one-half of the army were not actually engaged in firing the houses in twenty places at once, while the other half were not quiet spectators, indifferently looking on, there might be some shrewdness in this suggestion," he wrote, with rage. "If it could be shown that the whiskey found its way out of stores and cellars, grappled with the soldiers and poured itself down their throats, they are relieved of the responsibility.

Only rubble was left of the old state house (left), which was destroyed at 4 a.m. on Saturday, February 18, but the new state house (on the right) was under construction and was only slightly damaged. Courtesy of the Irvin Department of Rare Books and Special Collections in the Ernest F. Hollings Special Collections Library at the University of South Carolina, Columbia, S.C.

"Why did the soldiers prevent the firemen from extinguishing the fire as they strove to do? Why did they cut the hose as soon as it was brought into the streets? Why did they not assist in extinguishing the flames? Why, with twenty thousand men encamped in the streets, did they suffer the stragglers to succeed in a work of such extent?"

Simms claimed that Sherman's army was under perfect discipline. "They were, as an army, completely in the hands of the officers," he said. "Never was discipline more complete—never authority more absolute."[467]

"That the fire was permitted, whether set by drunken stragglers or negroes, to go on, and Sherman's soldiers prevented, by their active opposition, efforts of the firemen, while thousands looked on in perfect serenity, seeming totally indifferent to the event." Simms said "quite sober" soldiers were seen in hundreds of cases busily engaged in setting fires and treating with violence the citizens who tried to stop the fires.

Federals threw brickbats and broke off part of the walking cane from the statue of George Washington. After it was repaired, local citizens wanted the part to be removed to forever show the true light of Sherman's troops. The repaired piece is at the S.C. Confederate Relic Room and Military Museum. Photo by Pat McNeely

"When entreated and exhorted by citizens to arrest the incendiaries and prevent the catastrophe, at the very outset, the officers, in many cases, treated the applicants cavalierly, and gave no heed to their application."

Simms said that during the raging of the flames, the act was justified by a reference to the course of South Carolina in originating the secession movement. Simms said the general officers held themselves aloof until near the close of the scene and of the night.

"That General Sherman knew what was going on, yet kept aloof and made no effort to arrest it, until daylight on Saturday, ought, of itself, to be conclusive," Simms said.

In final rage, Simms said that, with his army under such admirable discipline, Sherman "could have arrested it at any moment; and that he did arrest it, when it pleased him to do so, even at the raising of a finger, at the tap of a drum, at the blast of a single trumpet.[468]

"But what need of these and a thousand other suggestive reasons, to establish a charge which might be assumed from a survey of Sherman's general progress, from the moment when he entered South

Although efforts were made to destroy the Mexican-American War monument on the State House grounds, it survived because it was guarded through the night by Federal soldiers. Photo by Pat McNeely

Carolina? The march of his army was a continued flame—the tread of his horse was devastation."[469]

Simms described the attitude of the northern press as they urged Sherman to wreak vengeance on South Carolina. "The Northern press furnished him the cri de guerre to be sounded when he should cross our borders. '*Vo victis!*'—woe to the conquered!—in the case of a people who had first raised the banner of secession. 'The howl of delight,' (such was the language of the Northern press) sent up by Sherman's legions, when they looked across the Savannah to the shores of Carolina, was the sure forerunner of the terrible fate which threatened our people should the soldiers be once let loose upon our lands," Simms said. "Our people felt all the danger."[470] When Sherman first sought to blame someone for his inebriated soldiers, he accused Governor Andrew McGrath, who had established the state government in Union, about 100 miles north of Columbia. Even when the Mixed Commission on American and British claims investigated the charges after the war in 1872, Sherman was saying that he had not ordered anyone to burn the city, which was true, according to his general orders. Although dozens of citizens would testify about the drunken out-of-control soldiers who had robbed, pillaged and burned their houses and possessions, the Commission would on March 30, 1872, vote against an award for the English claimants.

Sherman sent the left wing to Alston, 25 miles north of Columbia, to cross the Broad River. Confederates burned the bridge to slow their entry into Fairfield County, but remnants of the old bridge can still be seen from this bridge when the water is low. Photo by Pat McNeely

Guns, shells and other military supplies were produced at the Palmetto Iron Works, which was destroyed on Saturday, February 18. The building still stands at the corner of Laurel and Lincoln streets and is owned by the City of Columbia. *Courtesy of the South Caroliniana Library at the University of South Carolina, Columbia, S.C.*

As the sun rose over the destruction in Columbia on Saturday, February 18, Dr. LeConte started on his way back from Alston, where the left wing would cross the Broad River. All LeConte's possessions, lecture notes, government documents and supplies had been captured by Sherman's soldiers and destroyed. Returning to Columbia, LeConte said, "I entered the city at the extreme northern end, and went down the whole length of the main street, a mile and a half. Not a house was standing, and I met not a living soul! The beautiful city ...sat desolate and in ashes. The fire had swept five or six blocks wide through its heart, leaving only the eastern and western outskirts. At last I saw the brick a wall surrounding the campus and the buildings of the College, and a few minutes later was knocking at the door of my own ivy-covered home."[471]

He listened with sorrow as his daughter Emma, who had kept a diary, and the rest of his family and friends described their night of terror. "Dr. Carter (one of the medical doctors in the hospitals on the college campus) says it was a touching sight to see the poor fellows trying manfully to nerve themselves to meet their fate. And there was the regiment ostensibly sent to extinguish the fire, calmly looking on without raising a finger, and the patriots on the streets themselves applying the torch. The hospital was saved by one Yankee Captain (Stone) and two men (LaBorde and Rivers)—yet it contained many of their own wounded soldiers. ... Why in many houses the very guards stationed to protect helped the soldiers in smashing and destroying. It is sickening to listen to the tale of distress, much more to try to write of it. A heavy curse has fallen on this town—from a beautiful bustling city it is turned into a desert."[472]

Wasting no time, Sherman began preparing to ride out of Columbia with his troops, so he tweaked his story one more time and claimed that his troops not only had had nothing to do with the fire but that he had "in fact saved what was left of the city."[473] In his official report, Sherman said that before one single building had been fired by his orders on Saturday, February 18, "the smoldering fires, set by Hampton's order, were rekindled by the wind, and communicated to the buildings around. About dark, they began to spread, and got beyond the control of the brigade on duty within the

The Confederate Printing Plant of Evans & Cogswell on Gervais Street was raided and destroyed, and Sherman's soldiers gambled wildly with the money they took from the building, which is a Publix today. Courtesy of South Carolinana Library at the University of South Carolina, Columbia, S.C.

city. The whole of Woods' division was brought in, but it was found impossible to check the flames, which, by midnight, had become unmanageable, and raged until about four a.m., when, the wind subsiding, they were got under control. I was up nearly all night, and saw Generals Howard, Logan, Woods and others laboring to save houses, and protect families thus suddenly deprived of shelter and bedding and wearing-apparel."[474]

Sherman's account left out the pillaging and robberies that had begun as the troops entered the city, the drunken soldiers who had slashed and set fire to the cotton, his order to Howard to replace drunken soldiers after he arrived, the guards who abandoned their posts so that houses and businesses could be robbed and burned, the destruction of Columbia's firefighting equipment, dozens of horror stories about the Federal soldiers who entered occupied houses with combustibles to torch the interiors, and eye-witness accounts of the robbing, pillaging and destruction throughout the city.

Because Sherman did not arrive in the city for almost two hours after the first soldiers arrived, he did not care that the cotton bales in the middle of Richardson (Main) Street were wet and soggy from an eight-hour rain the night before and that the cotton bales had to be slashed open before they could be set on fire. As the Reverend Shand reported, the drunken soldiers had danced around the bales of cotton with lit cigars and had set the first cotton fires in the street. Before Sherman arrived, a fire in the prison had also been set and the prisoners escaped.

By the time Sherman arrived, the wind was blowing, cotton was flying in the streets from the slashed bales, and Stone and his men were busy trying to put out cotton fires and the fire inside the prison at Washington and Assembly. Therefore, Sherman's account of seeing cotton burning in the street on his arrival was accurate. When Sherman was casting around on Saturday, February 18, for someone to blame instead of his drunken soldiers, he "mystified the enemy," as he called it, by blaming the conflagration on Hampton, not only to take the blame off his own soldiers but also to continue his war on civilians.

Sherman admitted in his memoirs that he had to order drunken soldiers replaced during his entry into Columbia, but he stuck by his final and official position that came in various configurations but always involved blaming Hampton and cotton burning in the streets with high winds spreading fires through the night.

He said: "I disclaim on the part of my army any agency in this fire, but, on the contrary, claim that we saved what of Columbia remains unconsumed. And without hesitation I charge General Wade Hampton with having burned his own city of Columbia, not with a malicious intent, or as the manifestation of a silly 'Roman stoicism,' but from folly and want of sense, in filling it with lint, cotton, and tinder. Our officers and men on duty worked well to extinguish the flames; but others not on duty, including the officers who had long been imprisoned there, rescued by us, may have assisted in spreading the fire after it had once begun, and may have indulged in unconcealed joy to see the ruin of the capital of South Carolina. During the 18th and 19th the arsenal, railroad depots, machine shops, foundries, and other buildings were properly destroyed by detailed working parties, and the railroad track torn up and destroyed down to Kingsville and the Wateree bridge, and up in the direction of Winnsborough."[475]

He would not publicly admit until he wrote his memoirs in 1875 that his accusations were part of his effort to make civilians lose faith in their government and in leaders like Hampton. And thus, on the morning of Monday, February 20, Sherman turned his back on the smoldering city as his troops headed north towards Winnsboro. To "mystify the enemy," he would claim that not only had he not ordered the destruction of the city (which was true) and had blamed the nearest Confederate by saying that Hampton had carelessly left cotton burning in the streets, but he added a final psychological assault on the prostrate city when he claimed that Columbians should be grateful to him because his "brave" soldiers had labored through the night and saved what was left of the city.

Sherman's troops would continue their march of destruction on Monday, February 20, pillaging and burning their way north toward Winnsboro while blaming Confederates for the atrocities committed in their path. Sherman's strategy was working exactly as he had planned. The Confederates left in the burned-out towns in his wake were destitute and demoralized.

Sherman's charges would be forever publicly and privately and vehemently denied by Hampton, who was camped 20 miles away in Ridgeway at least seven hours before the fires began, but the victorious Sherman set the agenda that became the public perception—that Hampton had burned his own city, his own houses and the houses of all his friends in Columbia. Sherman's "mystify the enemy" campaign was working, and it was a public relations coup.

In defense of Hampton, the Reverend Shand said, "I heard no intimation from any quarter during the stay of the army that the crime was perpetrated by our own people. All believe it to be the work of the soldiers and determined upon by them before their occupation of the city. Some of them in my presence acknowledged the fact. When escaping from my house, I was met by one of them who accursed my grey hairs and pointing to the shocking scenes around us with great apparent exultation, exclaimed that he wanted our hearts' blood and desired to have every house burned and the city sowed in salt. 'We have taught them by this lesson,' said another, referring to the burning, and expressions of similar import were made by others of them of which I was cognizant."[476]

Felix Gregory de Fontaine
Courtesy of Tony and Maryjane Islan

Even though the Trinity parsonage had been burned and Sherman "had done us a fearful and lasting wrong, a wrong which has since, from its effects, carried numbers of our community to their graves," the Reverend Shand said, "neither my age nor my office—neither the precepts of our blessed religion, nor the natural temperament with which God has endowed me, incline me to exercise feelings of malice or unforgiveness towards him, nor to wish otherwise than that he may obtain forgiveness from Heaven."[477]

In later years in 1867, after Howard became head of the Freedmen's Bureau, he visited with Governor James L. Orr. Also present at the time was General R. K. Scott,[478] and Felix Gregory de Fontaine, who was a reporter for the *Charleston Courier* and owner of the *Daily South Carolinian* in Columbia and the South's most respected war correspondent. During that conversation, Howard admitted before five witnesses that Sherman's troops had set fire to the city. "It is useless to deny that our troops burnt Columbia, for I saw them in the fact," he said.[479]

However, when asked during a hearing in Washington in 1872: "Did you admit or state, in the course of that conversation, who destroyed Columbia on the night of the 17th of February, 1865?" Howard replied, "Yes, sir; I think I stated that the Confederate troops set it on fire."

Q. That the Confederate troops set it on fire?
A. Yes, sir, I think so; that was the matter of discussion between us.
Q. You did not admit that it was the Federal troops, excited by drink, that did it?
A. I may have said this: that doubtless men excited by drink set fires.
Q. But not your men?
A. I didn't say our men set them.
Q. You did not state, then or at any other time, that it was your belief that the United States soldiers set fire to Columbia; you positively swear that?
A. I do not wish to make a direct answer to that question, because," he said, he "thought some of that crowd were stragglers in which were soldiers from different parts of the army that had come into the town and from the jails to set fires."[480]

When Howard was questioned about the destruction of barns, cotton-gins, mills, machinery or any property of that nature, destroyed upon plantations on his line of march, he said, "I do know of it," and he admitted that there was a "quite considerable" amount destroyed. He also admitted that "a very large number of houses of private citizens were destroyed during the march." When asked if the troops of the United States destroyed the property, he said, "That I do not know, but I presume so; by soldiers." When asked to clarify, "You presume they were destroyed by the troops of the United States," he said, "Yes, sir."[481]

Stone, who was the first to enter the city, said in later years that the city was destroyed by "drunken troops of the United States," but not on anybody's orders. In addition to Sherman's accusations of blame against Hampton, Sherman had in Atlanta covered himself with a cloak of immunity by issuing orders for his soldiers that contained enough leeway to steal all livestock and poultry, horses and mules, forage, jewelry, valuables and clothes, while burning every chicken coop, private house and plantation along with the usually destroyed government buildings and arsenals with the full expectation of being welcomed back into camp as heroes.[482]

In later years, the Federals continued to deflect blame from their own drunken soldiers with tales that were frequently outlandish but in line with the blame-the-nearest-Confederate technique that Sherman used all through his campaign. Captain W. H. Goodrell, Company B, 15th Iowa Infantry, would go so far as to say in a letter that he wrote at the request of Sherman and sent to the *New York Times* that he saw a resident of the city of Columbia set his own house on fire. "A German, who was a resident of Columbia, and, therefore, a citizen of the Confederacy, set fire to his own building, saying that he did it for the purpose of revenging himself on the rebels for what they had made him suffer, and by burning his own house he would cause the burning of many others."[483]

It was a pattern of destruction that was never officially ordered by Sherman but was universally blamed on somebody else—usually Confederates. Even Howard, who on several occasions admitted that drunken soldiers burned Columbia, practiced deflection. When asked about the destruction of Pocotaligo, Howard said, "You know that generally when our troops destroyed private property, they were not ordered to destroy it." And Howard agreed that the private property was destroyed on the line of march and by offshoots from the main army, but also, he said by army followers and "army preceders," the code word for foragers.[484]

15 'HAVING UTTERLY RUINED COLUMBIA ...'

"The burning of the private dwellings, though never designed by me, was a trifling matter compared to the manifold results that soon followed. Though I never ordered or wished it, I have never shed tears over the event, because I believe it hastened what we all fought for, the end of the war."

—William T. Sherman

Rumors started circulating at 6 a.m. on Monday, February 20, that Hampton had attacked the advance of Sherman's army at Killian's mills, ten miles north of Columbia. Sherman hurriedly issued orders, and the army marched out of Columbia at 8 a.m., sparing some of the establishments that had been doomed to destruction.[485]

Believing that Sherman would head north to Charlotte, Beauregard had withdrawn his troops through Rock Hill to concentrate his decreasing military strength in Mecklenburg County, North Carolina, and Hardee, who had evacuated Charleston on February 18, had retreated through Cheraw toward Salisbury, North Carolina.[486]

"Having utterly ruined Columbia," Sherman wrote, the Federals resumed their march across South Carolina on February 20. His strategy was working, and he was well pleased. He would testify before the Mixed Commission on March 30, 1872, that the ulterior and strategic advantages "of the occupation of Columbia are seen now clearly by the result."[487]

In line with his philosophy of "total war," Sherman not only showed no remorse about the burning of Columbia, he believed that the destruction of Columbia hastened the end of the war. Those looking for remorse from Sherman would never find it.[488] He had clearly described his strategy for the campaign through Georgia and the Carolinas, even warning that it would be "brutal and barbaric," and as for the burning of Columbia, he said, "The burning of the private dwellings, though never designed by me, was a trifling matter compared to the manifold results that soon followed. Though I never ordered or wished it, I have never shed tears over the event, because I believe it hastened what we all fought for, the end of the war."[489]

Sherman was very clear about his feelings—or lack of feelings—about Columbia. "If I had made up my mind to burn Columbia I would have burnt it with no more feeling than I would a common prairie dog village; but I did not do it." And in spite of dozens of eye-witnesses who had tried to save their homes, churches and businesses from the torches of Federal soldiers, Sherman said, "I saw no soldier engaged in any act of conflagration except this young man who appeared to be drunk.... He was behaving badly; he was the man whom my aide-de-camp shot and brought to me; I saw no soldier engaged in any act of incendiarism that night."[490]

Even the pleas to save the water works failed, although when the mayor begged for some food for those who had survived the fire, Sherman left 560 head of broken down and dying cattle on the college green inside the brick walls of South Carolina College. It was not, however, an act of generosity since the cattle were "such as were not able to be driven any further," Gibbes said.[491] And further, no forage had been left for the cattle, and no water was available since the water-works had been destroyed, and "it was impossible to drive them to the river."[492] And, in spite of their pleas, Sherman ordered the gas works to be destroyed before he left. His only concession to their fervent pleas was to leave Young's (grist) Mill still standing.[493]

Columbia citizens held a meeting and decided to butcher the cattle; so, twenty or thirty volunteers began slaughtering the animals as fast as they could. "Even killing them as rapidly as possible, one hundred and sixty of the number died before they could be killed," Gibbes said. The poor, tough beef plus 100 barrels of salt that had been found in the basement of the capitol was all that was left to feed 20,000 people.[494]

An old shed at the corner of Plain (Hampton) and Market (Assembly) streets that escaped the flames was turned into a market or ration house, and for weeks it was the gathering place for the rich and poor. "Here rations of tough beef and salt were given out," Gibbes said. "Those who were able to pay paid; those who could not were supplied gratuitously; but all were allowanced, and that to what was barely sufficient to feed their families, every one having to testify as to the number of mouths he had to fill."[495]

Gibbes said the character of the beef, which at first seemed to be a great misfortune, turned out to be a blessing. "Had it been good, fat meat, it would have been, comparatively, a drop in the bucket toward supplying our necessities, but, fortunately, its quality compensated for its quantity, and I am certain that the survivors of that time will always preserve a lively recollection of the tough, blue sinews that, like India rubber, the more you chewed it the larger it got."[496]

The only other food that Columbians would have for two weeks after Sherman left was the loose corn picked up from the ground where the horses of the Federals had fed. Those who could leave town started walking toward Augusta, Newberry and other neighboring towns because no means of transportation had been left in Columbia.[497]

With smoke still rising from the ashes in Columbia, Sherman said, "The right wing began its march northward toward Winnsboro, on the 20th, which we reached on the 21st, and found Slocum, with the left wing, who had come by the way of Alston. Thence the right wing was turned westward, toward Cheraw. and Fayetteville, North Carolina, to cross the Catawba River at Peay's Ferry."[498]

As they followed the railroad to Ridgeway and Winnsboro, foragers, as usual, ranged ahead and beside them, confiscating animals, crops and forage, and troops lagged behind to destroy the tracks. As they passed by Jenkinsville, Federals damaged the rock wall that had been built in 1852 around the Old Brick Church.[499]

While camped in Winnsboro, Myers wrote the letter on February 26, 1865, to his wife in Boston that described in detail the regulations of robbing and stealing valuables and the way the plunder was divided in Sherman's army. Myers implicated Sherman in the division of loot. The details of the letter are supported by stories from hundreds of citizens in Columbia who had been violently robbed of all valuables and jewelry.

Myers wrote:

My Dear Wife: I have no time for particulars. We have had a glorious time in this State. Universal license to burn and plunder was the order of the day. The chivalry have been stript of most of their valuables. Gold watches, silver

pitchers, cups, spoons, forks, etc., etc., are as common in camp as blackberries. The terms of plunder are as follows:

The valuables procured we estimate by companies. Each company is required to exhibit the result of its operations at any given place. One-fifth and first choice falls to the share of the Commander-in-chief and staff, one-

Sherman's soldiers made William F. DeSaussure "fork over liberally" and burned his law office on Washington Street in downtown Columbia.
Courtesy: City of Columbia, S.C.

fifth to field officers of regiments, and three-fifths to the company. Officers are not allowed to join these expeditions without disguising themselves as privates. One of our corps commanders borrowed a suit of rough clothes from one of my men and was successful in this place; he got a large quantity of silver, (among other things, an old time silver milk pitcher) and a very fine gold watch from a Mr. DeSaussure at this place. DeSaussure is a F.F.V. [First Families of Virginia], of South Carolina, and was made to fork over liberally. Officers over the rank of Captain are not made to put their plunder in the estimate for general distribution. This is very unfair, and for that reason, in order to protect themselves, subordinate officers and privates keep back everything that they can carry about their person, such as rings, ear-rings, breast-pins, etc., of which, if ever I live to get home, I have about a quart—I am not joking—I have at least a quart of jewelry for you and all the girls, and some No. 1 diamond rings and pins among them.[500]

Gen. Sherman has silver and gold enough to start a bank. His share in gold watches and chains alone at Columbia was two hundred and seventy-five ($275), (which in today's dollars would be worth about $4,125),[501] but I said I could not go into particulars. All the general officers and many privates had valuables of every description, even to ladies' embroidered handkerchiefs. (I have my share of them, too. We took gold and silver enough from the d___d rebels to have redeemed their infernal currency twice over. This, (the currency) whenever we come across it we burn as we consider it utterly worthless. I wish all the jewelry this army has could be carried to the old Bay State. It would deck her out in glorious style, but alas! it will be scattered all over the North and Middle States. Thomas G. Myers, Lieut., etc.

The d____d negroes, as a rule, prefer to stay at home, particularly after they found out that we only wanted able bodied men (and to tell you the truth, the youngest and best looking women). Sometimes we take off whole families and plantations of negroes by way of repaying the secessionists' but the useless part of these we soon manage to loose—sometimes in crossing rivers—sometimes in other ways.[502]

"I shall write to you again from Wilmington, Goldsboro, or some other place in North Carolina. The order to march has arrived, and I must close hurriedly.

"Love to Grandmother and Aunt Charlotte. Take care of yourself and the children. Do not show this letter out of the family.
Your affectionate husband,
Thomas G. Myers, Lieut., etc.

P.S. I will send this by flag of truce to be mailed unless I have a chance to send it to Hilton Head. Tell Sallie I am saving a pearl bracelet and ear-rings for her; but Lambert got the necklace and breast-pin of the same set. I am trying to trade him out of them. These were taken from the Misses Jamieson, daughters of the President of the South Carolina Secession Convention. We found them on our trip through Georgia.[503]

The Misses Jamieson to whom Myers referred were the daughters of General David Flavel Jamison of Orangeburg, president of the Secession Convention. The daughters had apparently fled to Georgia where their jewelry was stolen, and their home was burned later as Sherman's troops went through Orangeburg.[504]

While Sherman and Howard were riding out of Columbia, Slocum and the left wing had reached Alston where they crossed the Broad River into Fairfield County. More than 500 head of starving and dying cattle were left in Columbia, and army rations, supplies and forage for the troops were getting scarce. The foragers, who were hungry for action, were already surging toward Winnsboro.

"General Slocum double-quicked the advance guard of his column into the village of Winnsboro to save the town from the torches of foragers," Conyngham wrote in *The New York Herald*. "General Pardee's brigade of Geary's division was in advance, and every effort was made to beat the stragglers from the Grand Army into town."

But they did not succeed. The town had been pillaged and robbed and set on fire by Sherman's foragers before the left wing arrived. "Generals Slocum, Williams, Geary, Pardee and Barnum all worked, burned their whiskers, and scorched their clothes to prevent the repetition of Columbia scenes.... and guards were posted in every house in town and other fires were quenched as they broke out."[505]

When Kilpatrick reached Chesterville (Chester) on Wednesday, February 22, he found that eighteen of his foragers had been "inhumanly, cowardly murdered... Two had their throat cut from ear to ear." He sent word to Wheeler that unless he could satisfactorily explain what happened to the men, he would execute eighteen of Wheeler's men who were being held prisoner.[506] Kilpatrick also apparently threatened to "burn every house" as far as his scouts extended because Wheeler mentioned it in his response.

Wheeler denied killing the foragers, saying that neither of his regiments was in any engagements on the day the bodies were found. "Should you cause eighteen of my men shot because you chance to find that number of yours dead, I shall regard them as so many murders committed by you and act accordingly... Your threat to 'burn

---

every house' as far as your scouts can extend is of too brutal a character for me, and, I think my government, to reply to."[507]

Although Kilpatrick released the prisoners he had condemned to execution, he was still skeptical and wrote back to Wheeler: "I am alive to the fact that I am surrounded by citizens, as well as soldiers, whose bitter hatred to the men I have the honor to command did not originate with this war, and I expect that some of my men will be killed elsewhere than on the battlefield; but I know, and shall not hesitate to apply, a sure remedy in each case."[508]

The bitter exchange between Kilpatrick and Wheeler, however, did not stop the pillaging and burning, and the foragers continued their wide swath of destruction.

Despite Wheeler's denial, Sherman complained to Hampton that some Federal foragers, or "bummers" as they had become known, had been shot out of hand by Confederate cavalry, and he accused Hampton of "murdering: after capture" Sherman's foraging parties. On February 24, Sherman wrote to Hampton:

"It is officially reported to me that our foraging parties are murdered after capture and labeled 'Death to all Foragers.' One instance of a lieutenant and seven men near Chesterville, and another of twenty from Feasterville. I have ordered a similar number of prisoners in our hands to be disposed of in like manner. I hold about 1000 prisoners captured in various ways, and can stand it as long as you: but I hardly think that these murders are committed with your knowledge, and would suggest that you give notice to the people at large that every life taken by them simply results in the death of one of your Confederates. Of course you cannot question my right to 'Forage on the Country.' It is a war right as old as history. The manner of exercising it varies with circumstances, and if civil authorities will supply my requisitions I will forbid all foraging. But I find no civil authorities who can respond to calls for

forage or provisions, therefore I must collect directly of the people.

"I have no doubt this is the occasion of much misbehavior on the part of our men, but I can not permit the enemy to judge or punish with wholesale murder. Personally I regret the bitter feelings engendered by this war, but they were to be expected, and I simply allege that those who struck the first blow and made war inevitable ought not, in fairness, to reproach us for the natural consequences. I merely assert our right to forage and my resolve to protect my foragers to the extent of life for life."[509]

Hampton denied knowledge of the incident mentioned, but angrily affirmed his order to shoot all Union troops engaged in burning private homes:

HEADQUARTERS,
In the Field, February 27, 1865.
Major General W. T. SHERMAN, U. S. Army:

GENERAL:
Your communication of the 24th instant reached me to-day. In it you state that it has been officially reported that your foraging parties are "murdered: after capture. You go on to say that you have "ordered a similar number of prisoners in our hands to be disposed of in like manner;" that is to say, you have ordered a number of Confederate soldiers to be "marked." You characterize your order in proper terms, for the public voice, even in your own country, where it seldom dares to express itself in vindication of truth, honor, or justice, will surely agree with you in pronouncing you guilty of murder if your order is carried out. Before dismissing this portion of your letter, I beg to assure you that for every soldier of

mine "murdered" by you, I shall have executed at once two of yours, giving in all cases preference to any officers who may be in my hands.

In reference to the statement you make regarding the death of your foragers, I have only to say that I know nothing of it; that no orders given by me authorize the killing of prisoners after capture, and that I do not believe my men killed any of yours, except under circumstances in which it was perfectly legitimate and proper that they should kill them. It is a part of the system of the thieves whom you designate as your foragers to fire the dwellings of those citizens whom they have robbed. To check this inhuman system, which is justly execrated by every civilized nation, I have directed my men to shoot down all of your men who are caught burning houses. This order shall remain in force so long as you disgrace the profession of arms by allowing your men to destroy private dwellings.

You say that I cannot, of course, question your right to forage on the country- "It is a right as old as history. " I do not, sir, question this right. But there is a right older, even, than this, and one more inalienable—the right that every man has to defend his home and to protect those who are dependent on him; and from my heart I wish that every old man and boy in my country who can fire a gun would shoot down, as he would a wild beast, the men who are desolating their land, burning their homes, and insulting their women.

You are particular in defending and claiming "war rights. " May I ask if you enumerate among these the right to fire upon a defenseless city without notice; to burn that city to the ground after it had been surrendered by the inhabitants who claimed, though in vain, that protection which is always accorded in civilized warfare to non-combatants; to fire the dwelling houses of citizens after robbing them; and to perpetrate even darker crimes than these - crimes too black to be mentioned?

You have permitted, if you have not ordered, the commission of these offenses against humanity and the rules of war; you fired into the city of Columbia without a word of warning; after its surrender by the mayor, who demanded protection to private property, you laid the whole city in ashes, leaving amidst its ruins thousands of old men and helpless women and children, who are likely to perish of starvation and exposure. Your line of march can be traced by the lurid light of burning houses, and in more than one household there is now an agony far more bitter than that of death. The Indian scalped his victim regardless of age or sex, but with all his barbarity he always respected the persons of his female captives. Your soldiers, more savage than the Indian, insult those whose natural protectors are absent.

In conclusion, I have only to request that whenever you have any of my men "murdered" or "disposed of," for the terms appear to be synonymous with you, you will let me hear of it, that I may know what action to take in the matter. In the meantime I shall hold fifty-six of your men as hostages for those whom you have ordered to be executed.

I am, yours, &c.,
WADE HAMPTON,
Lieutenant-General[510]

Neither Sherman nor Hampton followed through with the execution of any prisoners, and the widespread foraging, pillaging and burning continued as Sherman headed for the North Carolina line.

The cavalry was ordered to follow the railroad north as far as Chester, and then to turn east to Rocky Mount, the point indicated for the passage of the left wing," Sherman said. "In person, I reached Rocky Mount on the 22nd, with the Twentieth Corps, which laid its pontoon bridge and crossed over during the 23d. Kilpatrick arrived the next day in the midst of heavy rain, and was instructed to cross the Catawba at once, by night, and to move up to Lancaster, to make believe we were bound for Charlotte, to which point I heard that Beauregard had directed all his detachments, including a corps of Hood's old army, which had been marching parallel with us, but had failed to make junction with, the forces immediately opposing us. Of course, I had no purpose of going to Charlotte, for the right wing was already moving rapidly toward Fayetteville, leaving General Davis, with the Fourteenth Corps, on the west bank. The roads were infamous, so I halted the Twentieth Corps at Hanging Rock for some days, to allow time for the Fourteenth to get over."[511]

When Sherman arrived in Rocky Mount, he pitched his tent in front of the James Barkley home. His officers had their quarters in the house. Sherman talked with the women in the house every day, but they were living in terror that he would have their house burned.[512] Because of the torrential rains, Sherman stayed for eight days at Rocky Mount at the Barkley home, waiting for the swollen waters of the Catawba River to subside. The house, which was also named Rocky Mount, was located a few miles south of Great Falls near the Rocky Creek Power plant in the northeast corner of Fairfield County.

"The arrival of Sherman's army at Rocky Mount was preceded by tales of terror, of plundering, the burning of homes, barns, gin houses and cotton, the killing of livestock and the laying waste of fields," according to the Barkleys. "A silver pitcher, buried in the green-house was found, and the walls were quickly demolished in search of more silver. The yard fence and a large supply house full of tobacco and other stores were burned the first night. The gin-house full of cotton seed, the barn and stables were in flames soon after the arrival of the Yankees. Mrs. Barkley and her family lived in terror during the eight days while the soldiers were there.[513]

The Confederates had been marching north on a parallel line with the Federals so when Kilpatrick arrived in Rocky Mount in the midst of the heavy rain, Sherman ordered him to feint toward Lancaster to pretend that they were headed for Charlotte. Sherman had heard that Beauregard had directed all his detachments in that direction, including a corps of Hood's old army;[514] so, he wanted to fool Beauregard again.

Even though Sherman remained for a few days in Rocky Mount, the 20th Corps resumed its advance on February 23 toward the Catawba River as it neared the border with North Carolina.[515] The cavalry, which had followed the railroad north as far as Chester before also turning east to Rocky Mount, also left for the point of passage for the left wing to cross the Catawba on a pontoon bridge.[516]

General Joe Johnston
Source: Library of Congress

As Sherman's troops were leaving Rocky Mount, some of Wheeler's men skirmished briefly. "One of the rebels chased a Yankee through the house," witnesses recalled. Bullet holes from the skirmish are still visible in the weather boarding of the house.[517]

On March 6 Kilpatrick crossed the Pee Dee River (known as the Yadkin in North Carolina, becoming Pee Dee as it crosses the state line) and stopped at Rockingham, North Carolina. The Confederates knew that Sherman might march northwest, possibly from Cheraw to Rockingham, and then through Charlotte, to fall upon the rear of Lee at Petersburg; or he might take a northeasterly course via Fayetteville, on the Cape Fear River, by which he would join the reinforcements of General John Schofield, ready for him there.[518]

Seeing the direction of Sherman's march, Beauregard marched toward Charlotte to meet the brigades of the Army of Tennessee as they arrived from Georgia. Hill was headquartered in Augusta, which lay in the line of march of these troops. The Confederates were forced to march through most of Georgia, from Macon, on foot and with neither wagons nor arms. They passed, unorganized, through all of South Carolina, as far as Chester.[519]

Sherman heard of the Confederate movement through South Carolina and became apprehensive, even though by then he easily could have sent Kilpatrick to waylay and capture them all.[520]

Concerned about what he considered Beauregard's "feeble health," Lee recommended to Davis that he be replaced by Johnston. The change of command came on February 22 and Beauregard, although outwardly cooperative and courteous to Johnston, was bitterly disappointed at his replacement, and on Saturday, February 25, Johnston assumed command of the Army of Tennessee, now reduced to about 25,000 men, including state militia mustering in the Carolinas.[521]

Heavy rains again slowed the advance of Sherman's troops and created a difficult crossing of the Wateree River at Liberty Hill. Sherman's troops pillaged and burned Camden, before heading toward Cheraw on March 1.[522]

On February 27, a mounted Union detachment led by Captain William Duncan faced a superior force of Confederate cavalry at the Battle of Mount Elon, three miles south of Mount Elon in what became Lee County in 1902. The Confederates were commanded by Colonel Hugh K. Aiken. After a sharp hand-to-hand fight, Captain Duncan was forced to fall back across Lynches River, but Colonel Aiken was killed in the battle.[523]

Tradition says that Federal occupation troops took the church bell from St. John's Academy and gave it to Pearl Street Methodist Episcopal Church, now the St. James United Methodist Church on Pearl Street, Darlington.[524]

By March 2, Sherman reached Chesterfield along with the 15th and 17th Corps. After skirmishing briefly with General Matthew Butler's cavalry, Sherman ordered his men to burn the courthouse, which had been designed by Robert Mills, but they also burned the Chesterfield Academy and started several other fires in the town.[525]

While in Chesterfield, General Sherman chose the "Craig House" (then occupied by W. E. Craig) as his headquarters. All of the records were destroyed. Sherman's men entered the G. K. Laney house, then under construction, and started a fire in the middle of the room.

The scars from the fire still remain to be seen in the old house. The people of Chesterfield buried their silver and other valuables to keep the Northern forces from stealing them. One family buried their silver in the horse stable where the horses dug it up many years later.

Sherman's troops marched out of Chesterfield on March 3, fording Thompson Creek, and heading toward Cheraw. They had destroyed everything, leaving nothing for the people to eat. Some people were living on the corn that was dropped when

Emma LeConte, the 17-year-old daughter of Dr. Joseph LeConte, lived with her family in what is now Lieber College on the S.C. College campus. An eye-witness to the destruction of Columbia, she recorded the details in a diary. Courtesy of the South Caroliniana Library at the University of South Carolina, Columbia, S.C.

the Yankee soldiers fed their horses, and one family lived for weeks on apples![526]

As Sherman's troops were marching out of Chesterfield on March 3, the first wagonloads of relief were beginning to arrive in Columbia.

Emma LeConte wrote:

"Last Friday (3rd) we received two pieces of good news. In the first place Dr. Pratt arrived with four wagons to our relief. Two hours after receiving father's letter he started. In that short time provisions were hastily collected and clothing for

father, Uncle John and Capt. Green—father has been wearing a pair of blue trousers taken from a dead Yankee soldier at the hospital and given him by one of the doctors.

The officers of the Nitre Bureau contributed, throwing in shirts, collars, socks, etc.,—When he got to Prof. Holmes in Edgefield that generous-hearted friend set to work and loaded up a wagon with bacon, corn, clothing, etc., and sent word we must all come to his home right away. Such friends in times like these of scarcity and selfishness are indeed to be appreciated. Dr. Pratt left so hurriedly that he did not even go home to bid his wife goodbye—only dispatched her a note. He says no one in Augusta has the slightest conception of the desolation here—they suppose that only Main Street was burned, and that, the Yankees said, was done accidentally by our own soldiers in destroying cotton! As soon as the state of things was better understood contributions poured in. Our necessities are supplied for the present and we need not now draw rations from the town as we have been doing ever since the fire. ... The mayor issues rations to 7000 people—all that is left of a population of about 30,000. The original population of 12,000 was enormously increased since the war by refugees and other sources."[527]

When Dr. Pratt arrived back in Columbia after gathering provisions, he told Emma that the "greater part of Winnsboro was destroyed and the whole of Lexington—in fact every town and village in their track."[528]

The Confederacy had established a naval yard a quarter of a mile northwest of Marion in Marion County at the Pee Dee River Bridge in 1863 on the banks of the Great Pee Dee River. Under the command of Lt. Van Renssalaer Morgan, a wooden gunboat, the C.S.S. Pee Dee was built. Launched in November 1864, the gunboat was burned to prevent its capture by Federal forces in March 1865.[529]

Sherman was making additional efforts to control the information being published by newspapers by assigning Federal editors at the two Savannah newspapers and the *Charleston Courier*. However, no newspaper was left publishing in Columbia. Selby, who had been a partner in the *Daily South Carolinian* was struggling in Columbia to start a new newspaper, the *Phoenix*, while de Fontaine published several issues of the *Daily South Carolinian* in Charlotte, before resuming publication in Chester.[530]

As Confederate government officials in Richmond began abandoning the Confederate capital, hundreds of documents were destroyed or shipped by rail toward South Carolina.

When de Fontaine arrived in Chester on March 5 with his newspaper equipment, he was able to rescue a wagonload of Confederate documents at the Chester Railroad Station. Among the items he saved were a copy of the provisional Confederate

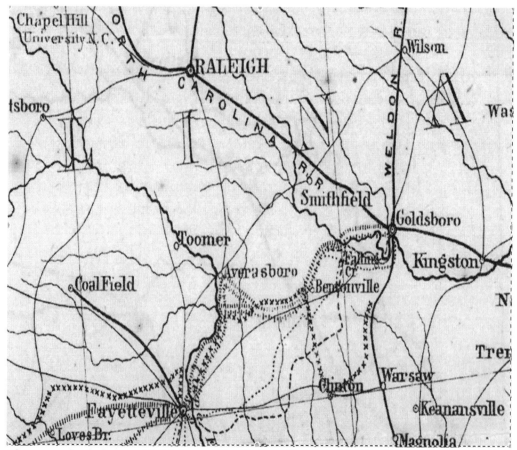

Sherman had chosen Goldsboro, North Carolina, as his final destination while he was still in Atlanta. *Source: Library of Congress*

constitution now at the Confederate Museum in Richmond, a permanent copy now at the University of Georgia, and documents belonging to the Confederate Attorney General now housed in the New York Public Library.[531]

Sherman's troops had reached Cheraw the day before on March 4 and Sherman established headquarters in a house belonging to a blockade-runner. General Howard's troops had crossed the Pee Dee on a pontoon bridge, and Mower's division skirmished with Confederates. Sherman had satisfied himself from inquiries that Hardee had come up from Charleston with only the Charleston garrison and that the Confederates were still scattered from Charlotte around to Florence behind him. He said, "I felt no uneasiness about the future, because there remained no further great impediment between us and Cape Fear River (North Carolina), which I felt assured was by that time in possession of our friends."[532]

Union forces occupied the home built by Dr. Edward W. Jones, a house built in 1826 that is located today at the corner of East Main and 121 South Marlboro Street in Bennettsville. The house was owned by Dr. J. Beatty Jennings when the Federals used it as their headquarters. The house was moved to its present location in 1905 and was opened by Marlboro County Preservation Commission as a house museum in 1976.[533]

Cheraw was full of goods that had been sent up from Charleston before the evacuation that could not be removed. Blair confiscated eight wagonloads of wine, including some of the "finest" madeira that Sherman said he had ever tasted, as well as loads of carpets that the officers and escort used for tent-rugs, saddle cloths and blankets. Sherman said Blair distributed the wine to the army generally, "in very fair proportions."[534]

An immense amount of stores were either confiscated or destroyed in Cheraw, including twenty-four guns, two thousand muskets and thirty-six hundred barrels of gunpowder. "By the carelessness of a soldier, an immense pile of this powder was exploded, which shook the town badly; and killed and maimed several of our men," Sherman wrote.[535]

The army had almost finished crossing the Pee Dee River by March 6 and was ready to resume the march on Fayetteville when

Federals found a copy of the *New York Tribune* in a house that had been Hardee's headquarters. The newspaper "contained a mass of news of great interest to us, and one short paragraph which I thought extremely mischievous," Sherman wrote. "I think it was an editorial, to the effect that at last the editor had the satisfaction to inform his readers that General Sherman would next be heard from about Goldsboro, because his supply vessels from Savannah were known to be rendezvousing at Morehead City:—Now, I knew that General Hardee had read that same paper, and that he would be perfectly able to draw his own inferences."[536]

Until that moment, "I had endeavored so to feign (sic) to our left that we had completely, misled our antagonists," Sherman said, "but this was no longer possible, and I concluded that we must be ready, for the concentration in our front of all the force subject to General Jos. Johnston's orders, for I was there also informed that he had been restored to the full command of the Confederate forces in South and North Carolina."[537]

On March 8, near the point where the Ebenezer Road crosses the Cheraw and Darlington Railroad, the 29th Missouri Mounted Infantry of Col. Reuben Williams' command deployed on either side of the tracks to capture a Confederate train approaching from Florence. The attempt failed when the engineer, discovering the trap, reversed his engine and escaped.[538]

De Fontaine resumed publication of the *Daily South Carolinian* on April 2, 1865, the same day that Richmond was evacuated by the Confederate government.[539]

General Edward E. Potter, who was commanding 2,700 Federal troops, left Georgetown on April 5, to destroy the railroad between Sumter and Camden. On April 16, the Skirmish at Spring Hill in Lee County was fought with Confederate militia under Col. James F. Pressley. After the skirmish, Federals camped at Spring Hill nearby. The McKinley Barfield home, which stood on the site, bore scars of the skirmishing on its walls.[540]

A small force of Confederate regulars and local Home Guard fought a defensive action on April 19 known as the Battle of Boykin's Mill in Kershaw County, nine miles south of Camden. The Confederates were able to delay the Federal advance for a day.[541]

16 ADVANCING INTO NORTH CAROLINA

"The people of South Carolina, instead of feeding Lee's army, will now call on Lee to feed them.

—*William T. Sherman*

Sherman and his troops were advancing on Fayetteville by March 8 and were expecting to be there by March 11 and then on to Goldsboro[542] where Sherman was planning to rendezvous with Schofield and his entire army. Sherman reported he had an abundance of all supplies, but would be foraging around Fayetteville for bread, sugar and coffee.

Sherman and the 15th Corps reached a little church called Bethel on March 9 and took refuge from a rain storm that forced them to corduroy all the roads. They reached Fayetteville on March 11, but found that Hardee and Hampton's cavalry had escaped across Cape Fear River and burned the bridge behind them. Hardee's troops had briefly captured the house where Kilpatrick and his brigade commander were staying and briefly held possession of the camp and artillery of his brigade. However, Kilpatrick and most of his men escaped into the swamp with their arms, reorganized and returned, catching Hampton's men, who in turn were scattered and driven away.[543]

Sherman said a group of his foragers, who, as usual, were "extemely bold and rash," had been caught by Hampton who "scattered them, killing some and making others prisoners." Sherman said, "Hampton got off with Kilpatrick's private horses and a couple hundred prisoners, of which he boasted much in passing through Fayetteville."[544]

When Sherman reached Fayetteville on March 12, he sent a letter to Stanton saying that Charleston, Georgetown and Wilmington "are incidents, while the utter demolition of the railroad system of South Carolina, and the utter destruction of the enemy's arsenals of Columbia, Cheraw and Fayetteville, are the principals of the movement. These points were regarded as inaccessible to us, and now no place in the Confederacy is against the army of the West. Let Lee hold on to Richmond, and we will destroy his country; and then of what use is Richmond. He must come out and fight us on open ground, and for that we must ever be ready. Let him stick behind his parapets, and he will perish."[545]

He said that at Columbia and Cheraw, "we destroyed nearly all the gunpowder and cartridges which the Confederacy had in this part of the country."[546]

When Sherman corresponded with Grant, he said, "Our march, was substantially what I designed—straight on Columbia, feigning (sic) on Branchville and Augusta. We destroyed, in passing, the railroad from the Edisto nearly up to Aiken; again, from Orangeburg to the Congaree; again from Columbia down to Kingsville on the Wateree, and up toward Charlotte as far as the Chester line; thence we turned east on Cheraw and Fayetteville. At Columbia we destroyed immense arsenals and railroad establishments, among which were forty-three cannon. At Cheraw we found also machinery and material of war sent from Charleston, among which were twenty-five guns and thirty-six hundred barrels of powder; and here we find about twenty guns and a magnificent United States' arsenal."[547]

Continuing his strategy of occupying no cities, Sherman said he couldn't afford to leave detachments, and he planned to destroy the arsenal in Fayetteville so the enemy would not have its use. "And the United States should never again confide such valuable property to a people who have betrayed a trust," he said.[548] He said the railroad from Charlotte to Danville, Virginia, was all that was left to the enemy.

Pleased with the destruction of the South Carolina supply lines to Lee, Sherman wrote to Major General Terry, commanding U.S. Forces in Wilmington, saying, "The people of South Carolina, instead of feeding Lee's army, will now call on Lee to feed them."[549] Sherman knew that Lee's supply lines had been further hampered by Sheridan's destructive cavalry raids in the Shenandoah Valley and could barely feed his own army.

As the starving and homeless people left in Sherman's wake struggled to find food and shelter, Sherman turned his attention to getting rid of as many as 30,000 freedmen and other refugees who had followed his army into Fayetteville. Sherman wanted to leave Fayetteville immediately, but he could not because he "wanted to clear my columns of the vast crowd of refugees and negroes that encumber us. Some I will send down the river in boats, and the rest to

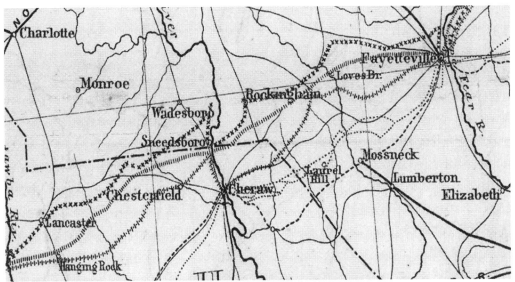

Sherman's troops moved through Hanging Rock, Lancaster, Chesterfield and Cheraw, South Carolina, on their way into North Carolina toward Fayetteville. Source: Library of Congress

Wilmington by land, under small escort, as soon as we are across Cape Fear River.[550] I must rid our army of from twenty to thirty thousand useless mouths; as many to go down Cape Fear (river) as possible, and the rest to go in vehicles or on captured horses via Clinton to Wilmington."[551]

Howard reported to Sherman that he had secured one of the Confederate steamboats below Fayetteville, and Slocum was securing two more known to be above the city. "We will load them with refugees (white and black) who have clung to our skirts, impeded our movements, and consumed our food."[552]

In a letter to General Alfred Terry, Sherman said, "We have swept the country well from Savannah to here, and the men and animals are in fine condition. Had it not been for the foul weather, I would have caught Hardee at Cheraw or here (Fayetteville); but at Columbia, Cheraw, and here, we have captured immense stores, and destroyed machinery, guns, ammunition, and property, of inestimable value to our enemy. At all points he has fled from us."[553]

Sherman said that Johnston might try to interpose between his troops in Fayetteville and Schofield about Newbern, but finally decided that Johnston would probably concentrate his scattered armies at Raleigh, and "I will go straight at him as soon as I get our men reclothed and our wagons reloaded." He asked Grant to "keep everybody busy, and let Stoneman push toward Greensboro or Charlotte from Knoxville; even a feint in that quarter will be most important." [554]

"In the meantime, I had dispatched by land to Wilmington a train of refugees who had followed the army all the way from Columbia, South Carolina, under an escort of two hundred men... so that we were disencumbered, and prepared for instant battle on our left and exposed flank."[555]

Thus unencumbered, Sherman's army crossed Cape Fear River on March 15 on the march toward Goldsboro and was 13 miles out on the Raleigh road when it skirmished briefly with Hardee's infantry, artillery and cavalry. Hardee had taken up a strong position at Averasboro, but by the next morning, he was retreating toward Smithfield. Sherman said he lost 12 officers and 65 men killed and 477 men wounded. The Confederates had left 68 wounded men, who were, along with the wounded Federals, carried to a nearby house that served as a field hospital.

"In person I visited this house while the surgeons were at work, with arms and legs lying around loose, in the yard and on the porch; and in a room on a bed lay a pale, handsome young fellow, whose left arm had just been cut off near the shoulder. ... He asked in a feeble voice, if I were General Sherman. He then announced himself as Captain Macbeth, whose battery had just been captured; and said that he remembered me when I used to visit his father's house, in Charleston. I inquired about his family, and enabled him to write a note to his mother, which was sent her afterward from Goldsboro." Sherman saw Macbeth again years later in St. Louis, where he was a clerk in an insurance office.[556]

Kilpatrick sent a prisoner back from the skirmish line who turned out to be Colonel Albert Rhett, former commander of Fort Sumter. "He was a tall, slender, and handsome young man, dressed in the most approved rebel uniform, with high jackboots beautifully stitched, and was dreadfully mortified to find himself a prisoner in our hands," Sherman wrote. Rhett had mistaken two of Kilpatrick's men for Hampton's men and had been captured without a fight.[557]

In later years, Sherman wrote that he thought Rhett was an editor in New Orleans who had fought a duel.

While Sherman was still in Averasboro, he received a letter from Grant saying that "Lee has depleted his army but very little recently, and I learn of none going south. Some regiments may have been detached, but I think no division or brigade. The determination seems to be to hold Richmond as long as possible."[558]

Grant said that he was sending him 5,000 more men, who were already on their way to join him. "My notion is, that you should get Raleigh as soon as possible, and hold the railroad from there back. From that point all North Carolina roads can be made useless to the enemy, without keeping up communications with the rear."[559]

From Averasboro, Sherman's left wing and Slocum turned east toward Goldsboro, the assembly point for Sherman's armies. With the 14th Corps leading, they were within 27 miles of Goldsboro and five miles from Bentonville when Sherman thought all danger was past and joined Howard and the right wing.[560]

A messenger arrived almost immediately saying that Slocum's army had run up against Johnston's whole army, which Johnston later said was 14,100 infantry and artillery. Not much against Sherman's 62,000 men, but Sherman's supplies were low and he thought Johnston had many more troops than he did, so Sherman issued orders to avoid a general battle. Sherman sent orders for Slocum to fight defensively from the west while the right wing approached Johnston's rear from the east.

The heaviest fighting at Bentonville was on March 19, but the skirmishing at Bentonville ended after three days, and Johnston's army retreated west. Sherman said in later years that if he had known how small Johnston's army was on March 21, he would have overwhelmed him instead of letting him go.[561]

Sherman, however, was eager to reach Goldsboro. "We have now been out six weeks, (since leaving Columbia) living precariously upon the collections of our foragers, our men dirty, ragged, and saucy, and we must rest and fix up a little," Sherman said. The skirmishing since Sherman had entered North Carolina, including Averasboro and Bentonville, had been deadly. "Our entire losses thus far (killed, wounded, and prisoners) will be covered by 2,500, a great part of which are, as usual, slight wounds. The enemy has lost more than double as many, and we have in prisoners alone fully two thousand."[562]

Sherman's troops rode toward Goldsboro, where his whole army was assembling on March 23 and March 24. Sherman notified Grant that rations and clothing were being replenished, and "I feel certain, from the character of the fighting, that we have got Johnston's army afraid of us. He himself acts with timidity and caution. His cavalry alone manifests spirit, but limits its operations to our stragglers and foraging parties. My marching columns of infantry do not pay the cavalry any attention, but walk right through it."[563]

Sherman said he could pretty clearly see how, "in one more move, we can checkmate Lee, forcing him to unite Johnston with him in the defense of Richmond, or to abandon the cause."[564]

Leaving his army to rest and regroup, Sherman left on a train for Morehead City where he boarded a small captured steamer and steamed up to Fortress Monroe on the morning of March 27. By mid-afternoon, Sherman was sitting with Grant, his family and staff who were occupying a group of huts at City Point, Virginia, on the bank of the James River.

Sherman visited Grant in his headquarters at City Point, Virginia. Source: Library of Congress

17 PRESIDENT LINCOLN'S LAST WISHES FOR THE SOUTH

Thus was concluded one of the longest and most important marches ever made by an organized army in a civilized country.
—William T. Sherman

After visiting with Grant for several hours, Sherman learned that President Lincoln was on board the steamer River Queen lying at the wharf at City Point, Virginia, on the bank of the James River.

"We walked down to the wharf, went on board and found Mr. Lincoln alone, in the after-cabin," Sherman said. "He remembered me perfectly, and at once engaged in a most interesting conversation. He was full of curiosity about the many incidents of our great march, which had reached him officially and through the newspapers, and seemed to enjoy very much the more ludicrous parts—about the 'bummers,' and their devices to collect food and forage when the outside world supposed us to be starving; but at the same time he expressed a good deal of anxiety lest some accident might happen to the army in North Carolina during my absence."

Sherman assured him that the army was in good camps in Goldsboro and that it would require several days of foraging to collect enough food for the march. "Having made a good, long, social visit, we took our leave and returned to General Grant's headquarters," Sherman said.[565] When they returned to quarters at City Point, Grant's wife wanted to know if they had seen Mrs. Lincoln. "'No,' said the general. I did not ask for her;' and I added that I did not even know that she was on board. Mrs. Grant said, 'Well, you are a pretty pair!' and said their neglect was unpardonable. Grant said they would call again the next day and make amends for their unintended slight."

The next day, after meeting with the principal officers of the Army and Navy, Sherman and Grant took a small tug from the wharf to visit the President again. When Grant asked about Mrs. Lincoln, the President went to her stateroom, returned and begged us to excuse her as she was not well."[566]

Grant told the president that Sheridan was crossing the James River from the north by a pontoon bridge below City Point and that he was going to strike the Southside and Danville Railroads, the only remaining supply lines for Lee.

"I also explain that my army at Goldsboro was strong enough to fight Lee's army and Johnston's combined, provided that General Grant could come up within a day or so; that if Lee would only remain in Richmond another fortnight, I could march up to Burkesville, when Lee would have to starve inside of his lines, or come out from his intrenchments (sic) and fight us on equal terms."[567]

Grant and Sherman agreed that one or the other would have to fight one more bloody battle—but it would be the last. "Mr. Lincoln exclaimed, more than once, that there had been blood enough shed, and asked if another battle could not be avoided," Sherman said. "I remember well to have said that we could not control that event; that this necessarily rested with our enemy; and I inferred that both Jeff. Davis and General Lee would be forced to fight one more desperate and bloody battle. I rather supposed it would fall on me, somewhere near Raleigh."[568]

Sherman asked the President what was to be done with the rebel armies when defeated. "And what should be done with the political leaders, such as Jeff. Davis, etc.," Sherman asked. "Should we allow them to escape, etc.? Lincoln said...all he wanted of us was to defeat the opposing armies, and to get the men composing the Confederate armies back to their homes, at work on their farms and in their shops."[569]

As for President Davis, Lincoln said he was hardly at liberty to speak his mind fully, but intimated that Davis ought to clear out, "escape the country," but it would not do for him to say so openly.[570]

Lincoln illustrated his meaning with a story. "A man once had taken the total-abstinence pledge. When visiting a friend, he was invited to take a drink, but declined, on the score of his pledge; when his friend suggested lemonade, which was accepted," Lincoln said. "In preparing the lemonade, the friend pointed to the brandy-bottle, and said the lemonade would be more palatable if he were to pour in a little brandy; when his guest said, if he could do so 'unbeknown' to him, he would 'not object.'" Sherman said he inferred from the illustration that Lincoln wanted Davis to escape "unbeknown" to him.[571]

Group portrait of the Confederate cabinet includes (seated L-R) Attorney General Judah P. Benjamin; Secretary of the Navy Stephen M. Mallory; Vice President Alexander Stephens; President Jefferson Davis; Postmaster General John H. Reagan; and Secretary of State Robert A. Toombs; and (standing L-R) Secretary of the Treasury C.S. Memminger and Secretary of War Leroy Pope Walker. Source: Library of Congress

Sherman said Lincoln assured him that in his mind he was all ready for the civil reorganization of affairs at the South as soon as the war was over. "He distinctly authorized me to assure Governor (Zebulon) Vance and the people of North Carolina that, as soon as the rebel armies laid down their arms, and resumed their civil pursuits, they would at once be guaranteed all their rights as citizens of a common country; and that to avoid anarchy the State governments then in existence, with their civil functionaries, would be recognized by him as the government de facto till Congress could provide others."[572]

Sherman was more than ever impressed by Lincoln's "kindly nature, his deep and earnest sympathy with the afflictions of the whole people, resulting from the war, and by the march of hostile armies through the South; and that his earnest desire seemed to be to end the war speedily, without more bloodshed or devastation, and to restore all the men of both sections to their homes."[573]

Goldsboro was the end of the campaign that Sherman had designed in Atlanta, and now he was anticipating reaching Grant's field of operations in April. As Richmond was falling on April 2, the Confederate president and his cabinet fled south through Virginia and the Carolinas to Georgia.

On April 5, Sherman was relaxing in Goldsboro, saying, "My army is now here, pretty well clad and provided, divided into three parts, of two corps each—much as our old Atlanta army was." He was making plans to move on in a few days and to open communications with Grant, but he was waiting for more supplies and the arrival of some men who were marching up from the coast.[574]

"Thus was concluded one of the longest and most important marches ever made by an organized army in a civilized country," Sherman wrote. "The distance from Savannah to Goldsboro is four hundred and twenty five miles, and the route traversed five large navigable rivers, viz., the Edisto, Broad, Catawba, Pedee, and Cape Fear, at either of which a comparatively small force, well-handled, should have made the passage most difficult, it not possible. The country generally was in a state of nature, with innumerable swamps, with simply mud roads, nearly every mile of which had to be corduroyed. In our route, we had captured Columbia, Cheraw, and Fayetteville, important cities and depots of supplies, had compelled the evacuation of Charleston City and harbor, had utterly broken up all the railroads of South Carolina, and had consumed a vast amount of food and forage, essential to the enemy for the support of his own armies. We had in mid-winter accomplished the whole journey of four hundred and twenty five miles in fifty days, averaging 10 miles per day, allowed ten lay-days, and had reached Goldsboro with the army in superb order, and the (supply) trains almost as fresh as when we had started from Atlanta."[575]

Sherman was prepared to resume the march to come within Grant's field of operations. He knew there was no force that could delay his progress, unless Lee could elude Grant at Petersburg and make junction with Johnston, and thus united meet Sherman alone. "I had no fear even of that event," he said.[576]

As Sherman headed for Raleigh, North Carolina, a train arrived with a letter from Governor Zebulon Vance asking for protection for the citizens of Raleigh.[577] Sherman was planning to move on Ashboro and Greensboro, to cut off Confederate retreat lines through Salisbury and Charlotte. He issued orders to stop destroying railroads, mills, cotton and produce. He said troops would be permitted to continue foraging, "only more care should be taken not to strip the poorer classes too closely."[578]

Sherman had received word that Anderson would raise the Federal flag over Fort Sumter at noon on April 14.[579] Anderson had been the officer in charge when Fort Sumter was attacked almost exactly four years before on April 12, 1861. But the flag would be lowered to half-mast the next day after word arrived about the assassination of President Lincoln.

Sherman accepted Johnston's surrender in this old farm house belonging to James Bennett near Durham, N.C. Photo by Pat McNeely

Sherman agreed to meet with Johnston on April 16 at a point midway between Durham and Johnston's rear at Hillsboro. As Sherman was preparing to board the train for Durham, a telegraph operator arrived asking him to wait for transmission of an important dispatch in cipher from Morehead City. "I held the train for nearly half an hour, when he returned with the message translated and written out. It was from Mr. Stanton, announcing the assassination of Mr. Lincoln, the attempt on the life of Mr. Seward and son, and a suspicion that a like fate was designed for General Grant and all the principal officers of the Government. Dreading the effect of such a message at that critical instant of time, I asked the operator if any one besides himself had seen it; he answered No!" Sherman asked him not to reveal the contents until he returned that afternoon.[580]

Sherman reached Durham, which was 26 miles away, and rode up Hillsborough road for about five miles to the farmhouse of James Bennett to begin negotiating the surrender from Johnston. When the two generals were alone, Sherman showed Johnston the dispatch about Lincoln's assassination and watched him closely.

"The perspiration came out in large drops on his forehead, and he did not attempt to conceal his distress," Sherman said. "He denounced the act as a disgrace to the age, and hoped I did not charge it to the Confederate Government. I told him I could not believe that he or General Lee, or the officers of the Confederate army, could possibly be privy to acts of assassination; but I would not say as much for Jeff. Davis, George Sanders and men of that stripe."[581]

Sherman said that he dreaded the effect the news would have on his soldiers. "I feared some foolish woman or man in Raleigh might say something or do something that would madden our men, and that a fate worse than that of Columbia would befall the place."[582]

As soon as Sherman reached Raleigh, he published orders for the army and announced the assassination of President Lincoln. "I doubt if, in the whole land, there were more sincere mourners over his sad fate than were then in and about Raleigh. I watched the effect closely, and was gratified that there was no single act of retaliation; thought I saw and felt that one single word by me would have laid the city in ashes, and turned its whole population houseless upon the country, if not worse.[583]

Major Henry Rathbone (left) lunges toward John Wilkes Booth (right) as he fires his gun at President Lincoln. Rathbone's fiancé Clara Harris (second from left) reacts in fear beside the President's wife. Source: Library of Congress

The news of President Lincoln's death produced a "most intense effect" on Sherman's troops. "At first I feared it would lead to excess; but now it has softened down, and can easily be guided," Sherman said. "None evince more feeling than General Johnston, who admitted that the act was calculated to stain his cause with a dark hue; and he contended that the loss was most serious to the South, who had begun to realize that Mr. Lincoln was the best friend they had."[584]

Sherman and his generals wanted to end the war and dreaded the long and harassing march in pursuit of a dissolving and fleeing army—"a march," he said, "that might carry us back again over the thousand miles that we had just accomplished....We discussed all the probabilities, among which was, whether, if Johnston made a point of it, I should assent to the escape from the country of Jeff. Davis and his fugitive cabinet; and some one of my general officers, either Logan or Blair, insisted that, if asked for, we should even provide a vessel to carry them to Nassau from Charleston."[585]

Fearing that the Confederates would disperse and begin guerrilla warfare, Sherman was eager to come to an agreement with Johnston and Hampton. As Sherman began meeting with the Confederate generals, he was unaware of orders that had been issued on March 3 forbidding Grant (and thus any of his subordinates) from any conferences with Lee (and thus any of his subordinates), and Sherman assumed that he had the right to negotiate proposed terms of surrender for submission to President Andrew Johnson.[586]

Recalling his conversation with President Lincoln at City Point, Sherman wrote terms of surrender to submit to President Johnson. When Johnston asked about the political rights of his men and officers after the surrender, Sherman said that "Mr. Lincoln's proclamation of amnesty, of December 8, 1863, (was) still in force." The proclamation enabled every Confederate soldier and officer below the rank of colonel to obtain an absolute pardon by simply laying down his arms and taking the common oath of allegiance. "General Grant, in accepting the surrender of General Lee's army, had extended the same principle to all the officers, General Lee included; such a pardon, I understood, would restore to them all their rights of citizenship."[587]

As the Confederate government began disintegrating, President Jefferson Davis and his cabinet fled south. He is shown riding with his escort over the Georgia Ridge five days before his capture on May 10. Source: Library of Congress

18 THE END OF THE CAMPAIGN—AND THE WAR

The bulletin from the Secretary of War gave warrant to the impression, which was soon broadcast, that I might be bribed by banker's gold to permit President Jefferson Davis to escape.

—*William T. Sherman*

While Sherman was preparing the proposed terms of surrender, Grant arrived in Raleigh and advised Sherman to accept Johnston's surrender on the same terms as his with Lee. So Sherman rode out to Bennett's house where he and Johnston signed the agreement on April 26. The agreement provided for the end of all acts of war and the surrender of all arms and public property and agreement for all offices and men to agree in writing not to take up arms against the U.S. government. Officers could keep side arms, and they would be permitted to keep private horses and baggage and return home.[588] The agreement provided for the Confederate armies to disband and deposit their arms and public property in the State Arsenal and for each officer and man to file an agreement to cease from acts of war.[589]

While Sherman and Johnston were negotiating in North Carolina, the body of Abraham Lincoln lay in state in the East Room and then in the Capitol Rotunda from April 19 through April 21. For the final journey with his son Willie, both caskets were transported in the executive coach "United States," and for three weeks the Lincoln funeral train decorated in black bunting chugged slowly across the country from Washington, D.C., to Springfield, Illinois. The train stopped at cities along the way for large-scale memorials attended by thousands of mourners.

Sherman thought often of Lincoln's words of praise and final advice at City Point and felt supremely satisfied with the results of his campaign through Georgia and the Carolinas. He knew how pleased Lincoln would have been with the impending surrender of the Confederate troops from Sherman's battlefields. Sherman ordered his troops to remain where they were with the cavalry occupying Durham's Station and Chapel Hill, Slocum's army at Aven's Ferry on Cape Fear River, Howard's men strung out along the railroad toward Hillsboro, and the rest of the army in Raleigh.

After Johnston signed the agreement,[590] Sherman turned it over to Grant.

Sherman's pride and satisfaction in his herculean campaign through the swamps and rivers of Georgia and the Carolinas was short-lived. The proposed terms of surrender fell into a quagmire of political maneuvering in Washington, D.C., and Sherman was notified by Halleck and Stanton on April 23 that the agreement had been rejected.

Even worse, the report on the rejection, which was published in the *New York Times* on April 24, implied that Sherman had opened a way for Jefferson Davis to escape to Mexico or Europe with his plunder when Sherman ordered General Stoneman to withdraw from Salisbury, North Carolina.

The dispatch said: "It is stated here, by respectable parties, that the amount of specie taken south by Jeff. Davis and his partisans is very large, including not only the plunder of the Richmond banks, but previous accumulations. They hope, it is said, to make terms with General Sherman, or some other commander, by which they will be permitted, with their effects, including this gold plunder, to go to Mexico or Europe. Johnston's negotiations look to this end."[591]

Sherman was livid. The bulletin from the Secretary of War "gave warrant to the impression, which was soon broadcast, that I might be bribed by banker's gold to permit Davis to escape," he said. "I regarded this bulletin of Mr. Stanton as a personal and official insult, which I afterward publicly resented."[592]

Sherman had not realized that before his assassination, Lincoln had ordered Grant to proceed to Sherman's headquarters in North Carolina and direct operations against the enemy.[593] Sherman said he had not known about the March 3 dispatch from Lincoln to Stanton that limited Grant and thus his subordinates to negotiations on purely military matters, even though at Savannah, Stanton had authorized Sherman to control all matters, civil and military. Stanton implied that Sherman had received a copy of the dispatch and had disobeyed orders. The newspaper article said that "General Sherman was ordered to resume hostilities immediately."[594]

In white-hot anger, Sherman wrote his old friend Grant on April 28. Sherman said he was furious that Stanton had taken his secret military communication with the cabinet to the newspapers but even more outraged that he was being publicly accused of disobeying orders, insubordination and of taking a bribe to open an escape path for Davis by ordering Stoneman out of Salisbury. "General Stoneman was not at 'Salisbury,' but had gone back to 'Statesville,'" Sherman said. "Davis was between us, and therefore Stoneman was beyond him. By turning toward me he was approaching Davis, and, had he joined me as ordered, I would have had a mounted force greatly needed for Davis's capture, and for other purposes. Even now I don't know that Mr. Stanton wants Davis caught, and as my official papers, deemed sacred, are hastily published to the world, it will be imprudent for me to state what has been done in that regard."[595]

Sherman lashed out at Stanton. "As the editor of the *Times* has (it may be) logically and fairly drawn from this singular document the conclusion that I am insubordinate, I can only deny the intention."[596]

In his letter to Grant, Sherman said he had never in his life "questioned or disobeyed an order, though many and many a time I risked my life, health, and reputation, in obeying orders, or even hints to execute plans and purposes, not to my liking."[597]

Sherman described his four years in camp in which "I conferred freely with the best officers in this army as to the points involved in this controversy.... They will learn with pain and amazement that I am deemed insubordinate, and wanting in commonsense; that I, who for four years have labored day and night, winter and summer, who have brought an army of seventy thousand men in magnificent condition across a country hitherto deemed impassable, and placed it just where it was wanted, on the day appointed, have brought discredit to our Government! I do not wish to boast of this, but I do say that it entitled me to the courtesy of being consulted before publishing to the world a proposition rightfully submitted to higher authority for adjudication, and then accompanied by statements which invited the dogs of the press to be let loose upon me."[598]

Sherman ended his letter to Grant on a bitter note. "I will therefore go on to execute your orders to the conclusion, and, when done, will with intense satisfaction leave to the civil authorities the execution of the task of which they seem so jealous."[599] And he demanded that his letter should be made public in the newspapers.

As Sherman prepared to head back to Savannah by sea to meet officers stationed at Macon and Augusta, Stanton issued a second dispatch on April 27 that included orders for Generals Edward R. Canby and George Henry Thomas to disregard Sherman's arrangements with Johnston and to "push the enemy in every direction."[600] The dispatch said that Jeff. Davis's money was moving south from Goldsboro in wagons as fast as possible. Thomas and Wilson were warned not to obey any orders from Sherman and, along with Canby and all commanders on the Mississippi, were to take measures "to intercept the rebel chiefs and their plunder."[601]

Sherman was outraged again. "By this time, I was in possession of the second bulletin of Mr. Stanton, published in all the Northern newspapers, with comments that assumed that I was a common traitor and a public enemy; and high officials had even instructed my own subordinates to disobey my lawful orders," even though Sherman's command over North Carolina had never been revoked or modified.[602]

Stanton was insinuating that Sherman was allowing Davis to escape with wagon loads of "specie ... estimated here at from six to thirteen million dollars."[603] Sherman was shocked and insulted by the tone of the dispatches coming out of Washington and the insinuation that Davis had enough money to buy his escape from Sherman's army.[604]

Rumors began circulating about the vast amounts of gold and silver that had been hauled out of Richmond as the Confederate government collapsed. "The assertion that Jeff. Davis's specie-train, of six to thirteen million dollars, was reported to be moving south from Goldsboro in wagons as fast as possible, found plenty of willing ears, though my army of eighty thousand men had been at Goldsboro from March 22d to the date of his dispatch, April 26th and such a train would have been composed of from fifteen to thirty-two six-mule teams to have hauled this specie, even if it all were in gold."[605]

Sherman was "outraged beyond measure" at the tone and substance of the published bulletins of the War Department. Being accused of allowing Davis to buy his freedom was an insult that

Sherman would never forgive or forget. Sherman would write years later in his memoirs that "some of it was paid to (Davis') escort, when it disbanded at or near Washington, Georgia, and at the time of his capture he had a small parcel of gold and silver coin, not to exceed ten thousand dollars, which is now retained in the United States Treasury-vault at Washington, and shown to the curious.[606]

"The thirteen millions of treasure, with which Jeff. Davis was to corrupt our armies and buy his escape, dwindled down to the contents of a hand valise," he wrote bitterly.

As Sherman watched the rising turmoil and confusion in Washington, he "then realized the national loss in the death at that critical moment of Mr. Lincoln, who had long pondered over the difficult questions involved, who, at all events, would have been honest and frank, and would not have withheld from his army commanders at least a hint that would have been to them a guide. It was plain to me, therefore, that the manner of his assassination had stampeded the civil authorities in Washington, had unnerved them, and that that they were then undecided as to the measures indispensably necessary to prevent anarchy at the South."[607]

As the war stumbled to an end, Sherman was beginning to believe that President Johnson was bitter and vindictive in his feelings toward the South, and he could see the "wild pressure of every class of politicians to enforce on their new President their pet schemes."[608]

Sherman summoned his army and corps commanders together on April 28 at his headquarters at the governor's mansion in Raleigh where he explained what had happened and distributed orders for the future. Schofield, Terry and Kilpatrick were to remain on duty in the Department of North Carolina, already commanded by Schofield, and the right and left wings were to march north by easy stages to Richmond, where they would wait for him to return from the south.

Sherman left by rail for Wilmington, where he boarded a steamer to Port Royal and Savannah to meet with emissaries from General James H. Wilson at Macon and to order supplies for troops at Macon and Augusta. On his return on May 2, Sherman boarded a steamer to return to North Carolina. As he passed South Carolina, "We went into Charleston Harbor, passing the ruins of old Forts

Moultrie and Sumter without landing," he said. He reached the city of Charleston, which was held by part of the division that he had left at Pocotaligo. "We walked the old familiar streets—Broad, King, Meeting, etc.,—but desolation and ruin were everywhere. The heart of the city had been burned during the bombardment."[609]

He inquired about his old friends, but they were all dead or gone, and he only saw a part of the family of Mrs. Pettigru, probably the family of J. L. Petigru, an outspoken opponent of nullification and secession. "I doubt whether any city was ever more terribly punished than Charleston, but, as her people had finally inaugurated the civil war by an attack on the small and devoted garrison of Major Anderson, sent there by the General Government to defend them, the judgment of the world will be, that Charleston deserved the fate that befell her."[610]

Sherman arrived back in Raleigh on May 9 to find that General Davis' 14th Corps had been ordered to be reviewed by Halleck. "This I forbade," Sherman said. "All the army knew of the insult that had been made me by the Secretary of War and General Halleck, and watched me closely to see if I would tamely submit. During the 9th I made a full and complete report of all these events, from the last report made at Goldsboro up to date, and the next day received orders to continue the march to Alexandria, near Washington."[611]

Sherman crossed over to Washington to meet with many friends—among them Grant and President Johnson. Both assured him that they had had nothing to do with the publication of Stanton's war bulletins. Sherman refused a reconciliation meeting with Stanton, "but, on the contrary, resolved to resent what I considered an insult, as publicly as it was made."[612]

Word arrived that President Jefferson Davis was captured near Irwinsville, Georgia, on May 10, and two weeks later on May 24, Sherman and Howard and all of Sherman's staff, rode slowly down Pennsylvania Avenue followed by Logan and the 15th Corps. All on the stand arose and saluted, and Sherman left his horse with orderlies and went upon the stand where he found his wife and their 8-year-old son Tom and her father. "Passing them, I shook hands with the President, General Grant, and each member of the cabinet," he said.

"As I approached Mr. Stanton, he offered me his hand, but I declined it publicly, and the fact was universally noticed."[613]

Sherman took his post on the left of the President and stood watching for 6 1/2 hours while his armies, the 14th, 15th, 17th and 20th Corps, passed in review. "Many good people, up to that time, had looked upon our Western army as a sort of mob," he said, "but the world then saw, and recognized the fact, that it was an army in the proper sense, well organized, well commanded and disciplined; and there was no wonder that it had swept through the South like a tornado."[614]

At the end of his campaign and the war, Sherman took his post on the left of the President to watch his victorious troops pass in review. Source: Library of Congress

INDEX

act of kindness, 18, 20

Aiken, South Carolina, 58, 63, 66, 67, 175, 182

Alston, South Carolina, 79, 156, 165, 168

Atlanta, 3, 5, 6, 7, 11, 15, 16, 18, 19, 20, 21, 22, 23, 24, 26, 29, 33, 34, 40, 42, 47, 70, 162, 190

Augusta, Georgia, 26, 27, 29, 30, 39, 40, 48, 49, 57, 59, 66, 67, 68, 76, 165, 174, 177, 182, 198, 199

Averysboro, North Carolina, 184, 185

Barnwell, South Carolina, 48, 62, 63, 65, 109, 110

Beaufort, South Carolina, 45, 48, 52, 54, 64, 65, 89, 92

Beauregard, P.G.T., 11, 24, 29, 36, 56, 57, 58, 68, 71, 76, 83, 88, 143, 146, 163, 173, 174, 175

Blair, Francis P., 52, 53, 61, 68, 179, 193

blame, 3, 4, 6, 22, 32, 104, 140, 142, 145, 146, 155, 158, 162

Bowties, Sherman's, 10

Brinkman, David, 85

Broad River, South Carolina, 48, 52, 83, 84, 85, 87, 88, 90, 91, 93, 156, 168

Bummers, 26

Calhoun, James M. Mayor, 19, 129, 142

Cape Fear River, North Carolina, 59, 174, 179, 181, 183, 184, 195

Catawba River, 46, 165, 173, 174

Charleston, South Carolina, 14, 23, 27, 28, 36, 38, 39, 40, 41, 45, 46, 49, 52, 53, 56, 57, 58, 59, 60, 61, 66, 67, 68, 71, 75, 76, 116, 132, 133, 137, 146, 148, 161, 163, 178, 179, 181, 182, 184, 190, 193, 199, 200

Chattanooga, 22, 34

Cheraw, South Carolina, 163, 165, 174, 175, 176, 179, 180, 181, 182, 183, 190

Chesnut, Mary Boykin, 58, 65

Chesterfield, South Carolina, 175, 176

Christ Episcopal Church, 130

City Hall, Columbia, 86, 100

City Point, Virginia, 8, 21, 34, 186, 187, 194, 195

Cobb, Howell, 29

Columbia, South Carolina, 1, 2, 3, 10, 13, 18, 27, 28, 38, 39, 48, 49, 50, 52, 54, 57, 58, 59, 61, 62, 65, 66, 68, 69, 70, 71, 73, 74, 75, 76, 77, 78, 79, 80, 82, 84, 85, 88, 89, 90, 92, 94, 101, 102, 104, 107, 108, 109, 110, 111, 114, 115, 116, 117, 120, 124, 125, 138, 140, 141, 142, 143, 144, 146, 147, 148, 149, 151, 155, 156, 157, 158, 159, 160, 161, 162, 163, 164, 165, 166, 168, 172, 176, 177, 178, 181, 182, 183, 184, 185, 190, 192

Confederate Printing Plant, 149

Congaree Creek, South Carolina, 70, 90

Conyngham, David, 73, 84, 90, 145, 146, 168

Coosawatchie, South Carolina, 39, 52

corduroyed, 50, 190

Corse, John M., 24

cotton, 3, 6, 7, 14, 38, 43, 48, 69, 74, 88, 97, 100, 103, 104, 114, 119, 127, 141, 142, 144, 146, 148, 158, 159, 161, 173, 177, 191

Daily South Carolinian, 49, 68, 72, 152, 161, 178, 180

Dalton, Georgia, 16

Davis, General Jefferson, 31, 44

Davis, General Jefferson Davis, 31

Davis, Jefferson President, 4, 11, 22, 58, 65, 75, 132, 173, 175, 188, 192, 193, 196, 197, 198, 199, 200

Dayton, L.M., 45

de Fontaine, Felix Gregory, 161

Duncan, Blanton, 2, 106, 107, 108, 109, 110, 175

Ebenezer Creek, Georgia, 31, 33, 44

Elmwood Avenue (the Upper Boundary), 84, 89, 113

England, 14, 57

Fairfield, South Carolina, 2, 46, 82, 168, 173

Fayetteville, North Carolina, 109, 165, 173, 174, 179, 181, 182, 183, 190

Federal, 5, 11, 12, 13, 14, 15, 21, 23, 24, 29, 30, 41, 44, 55, 61, 63, 66, 71, 72, 74, 84, 91, 95, 97, 104, 113, 115, 118, 120, 122, 126, 127, 133, 140, 148, 152, 158, 161, 169, 175, 177, 178, 180, 191

Finlay Park, previously known as Sidney Park, 133

First Baptist Church, 130

foragers, 9, 10, 14, 22, 26, 35, 51, 64, 90, 162, 165, 168, 169, 170, 171, 181, 185

Frazier, Garrison, 44

Garner's Ferry Road, 148

Georgia, 1, 2, 3, 4, 5, 8, 10, 16, 19, 21, 22, 23, 24, 25, 29, 30, 34, 35, 38, 42, 57, 68, 77, 109, 115, 163, 167, 168, 174, 179, 190, 195, 196, 199, 200

Gervais Street Bridge (also known as Congaree Bridge, 85, 106, 108, 109, 110, 113, 119

Gibbes, James G., 113, 121, 122, 124, 125, 126, 142, 164, 165

Gibbes, Robert W., 121, 123, 124, 128

Glover, Judge Thomas W., 70

Goldsboro, North Carolina, 49, 50, 59, 114, 167, 180, 181, 184, 185, 186, 187, 188, 190, 198, 200

Goodrell, W.H., 162

Goodwill Plantation, 148

Goodwyn, Mayor Thomas Jefferson, 73, 86, 88, 89, 93, 103, 106, 108, 109, 110, 112, 113, 115, 127, 140, 142

Governor's Mansion, 80, 112, 149

Grant, Ulysses S., 8, 20, 21, 23, 24, 26, 33, 34, 36, 38, 39, 40, 57, 59, 182, 184, 185, 186, 187, 188, 190, 192, 194, 195, 196, 197, 200, 207

Halleck, Henry, 20, 38, 42, 43, 144, 196, 200, 207

Hampton, Wade III, 3, 4, 30, 58, 59, 65, 71, 72, 86, 88, 91, 104, 108, 109, 110, 111, 116, 120, 121, 125, 126, 141, 142, 144, 146, 148, 152, 157, 158, 159, 160, 162, 163, 164, 169, 170, 172, 181, 184, 194

Hardee, William J., 16, 29, 30, 36, 57, 59, 75, 76, 77, 163, 179, 180, 181, 183, 184

Hardeeville, South Carolina, 47, 48, 51

Hazen, William B., 34, 82

Heyward, Pauline DeCaradeuc, 66

Hood, John Bell, 8, 15, 16, 17, 18, 19, 20, 21, 22, 23, 29, 41, 59, 66, 70, 173, 174

Hood, John Bell, 21

Howard, Oliver, 10, 25, 38, 48, 52, 64, 83, 90, 92, 93, 94, 101, 102, 104, 110, 114, 115, 116, 119, 138, 139, 140, 141, 145, 148, 158, 161, 162, 168, 179, 183, 185, 195, 200

Jacksonville, Florida, 45, 46

Johnson, President Andrew, 4, 46, 66, 67, 194, 199, 200

Johnston, Joseph, 16, 175, 180, 183, 185, 186, 188, 191, 192, 193, 194, 195, 196, 198

Kentucky, 16, 17, 108

Kilpatrick, Judson, 25, 48, 50, 63, 65, 66, 67, 77, 95, 168, 169, 173, 174, 175, 181, 184, 199

kindness, 20, 21, 126

LaBorde, Maximillian, 134, 136, 139, 157

LeConte, Dr. Joseph LeConte, 77, 78, 79, 108, 114, 136, 156, 176

LeConte, Emma LeConte, 134

Lee, Robert E., 7, 8, 21, 58, 59, 60, 82, 133, 174, 175, 180, 181, 182, 185, 186, 188, 190, 192, 194, 195

Lincoln, Abraham, 8, 13, 17, 22, 23, 32, 33, 37, 38, 46, 57, 58, 85, 149, 187, 188, 189, 192, 193, 194, 195, 196,

199

Logan, John A. "Black Jack", 92, 110, 119, 120, 144, 148, 158, 193, 200

Lyon, Judge Richard F., 25

McKenzie, John, 73, 88

McLaws, Lafayette, 30, 54, 61, 62

Midway, South Carolina, 64

Milledgeville, 10, 22, 23, 29, 38

Millwood, 111

Missouri, 17, 73, 74, 145, 180

Mixed Commission on British and American Claims, 14

Mower, Joseph A., 61, 68, 179

Myers, 13, 28, 29, 165, 167, 168

mystified the enemy, 10, 158

mystifying the record, 14

Nevins, Alan, 51

Nichols, George, 61, 74, 75, 118

North Carolina, 7, 24, 28, 33, 38, 39, 40, 49, 50, 59, 65, 109, 163, 165, 167, 172, 174, 179, 180, 185, 187, 189, 191, 195, 196, 198, 199

O'Connell, the Reverend Lawrence P. O'Connell, 129

Orangeburg, South Carolina, 62, 65, 68, 69, 70, 146, 168, 182

Pee Dee River, South Carolina, 174, 177, 179

Pensacola, Florida, 27

Petersburg, Virginia, 8, 21, 58, 174, 190

Pettigru, J.L., 200

Phoenix, 150, 178

Pocotaligo, South Carolina, 9, 39, 47, 48, 52, 53, 61, 162, 200

Port Royal, South Carolina, 27, 36, 46, 48, 199

Porter, the Reverend A. Toomer, 52, 137, 138

Poyas, 109

Purysburg, South Carolina, 51

Raleigh, 3, 6, 28, 59, 60, 183, 184, 185, 188, 191, 192, 195, 199, 200

reporters, 12

Richardson Street, or Main Street, 98, 103, 113, 125, 129, 139, 144, 158

Richmond, Virginia, 8, 26, 30, 39, 42, 59, 60, 73, 178, 180, 181, 185, 186, 188, 190, 196, 198, 199

Riverbanks Zoo, 74

Roanoke, North Carolina, 28, 40

Salkehatchie River, South Carolina, 57, 61, 62

Saluda River, 74, 82, 83, 84, 90, 125

Sandersville, Georgia, 29, 30

Savannah, Georgia, 8, 10, 13, 23, 24, 27, 29, 30, 31, 34, 36, 37, 38, 39, 40, 41, 42, 43, 44, 45, 46, 48, 50, 51, 52, 59, 61, 73, 90, 102, 114, 115, 155, 178, 180, 183, 190, 196, 198, 199

Schofield, John, 174, 181, 183, 199

Shand, the Reverend Peter, 98, 99, 100, 104, 116, 132, 143, 144, 158, 160

Sheldon ruins, South Carolina, 54

Sherman, William T., 1, 2, 3, 4, 5, 6, 7, 8, 9, 10, 11, 12, 13, 14, 15, 16, 17, 18, 19, 20, 21, 22, 23, 24, 25, 26, 28, 29, 30, 31, 32, 33, 34, 35, 36, 37, 38, 39, 40, 41, 42, 43, 44, 45, 46, 47, 49, 50, 51, 52, 53, 54, 56, 57, 58, 59, 61, 62, 64, 65, 66, 67, 68, 70, 71, 72, 73, 77, 78, 80, 83, 84, 87, 88, 89, 90, 91, 92, 97, 99, 101, 102, 103, 104, 105, 106, 107, 108, 109, 110, 112, 113, 116, 117, 118, 119, 120, 121, 129, 132, 133, 137, 138, 139, 140, 141, 142, 143, 144, 145, 146, 147, 148, 149, 150, 151, 152, 153, 154, 155, 157, 158, 159, 160, 161, 162, 163, 164, 165, 166, 168, 169, 172, 173, 174, 175, 176, 178, 179, 180, 181, 182, 183, 184, 185, 186, 187, 188, 189, 190, 191, 192, 193, 194, 195, 196, 197, 198, 199, 200, 201, 207

Sidney Park, later called Finlay Park, 133, 148

Simms, William Gilmore, 49, 55, 62, 65, 68, 71, 72, 73, 74, 75, 80, 85, 86, 87, 91, 94, 95, 97, 100, 104, 105, 107, 108, 109, 112, 113, 117, 120, 127, 128, 129, 130, 133, 138, 139, 140,

141, 144, 150, 151, 152, 153, 154
Slocum, 25, 48, 50, 65, 77, 80, 165, 168, 183, 185, 195
Sorghum, Camp, 83
South Carolina College, later known as the University of South Carolina, 77, 110, 134
St. Peter's Catholic Church, 120
Stanley, W.B., 73, 117
State House, 80
Stone, Charles, 54, 55, 85, 88, 89, 90, 93, 94, 95, 97, 102, 103, 104, 117, 138, 139, 140, 157, 158, 162
Stoneman, George, 184, 196, 197
Surrender Stone, 89
Tennessee, 5, 8, 15, 22, 23, 41, 56, 174,

175
Timrod, Henry, 68, 73
total war, 19, 20, 29, 163
Treasury, U.S., 14, 29, 37, 110, 128, 199
Trenholm, George A., 93, 110
Trezevant, Dr. Daniel H., 144, 145
Wheeler, Joseph, 23, 29, 31, 32, 42, 44, 51, 52, 54, 59, 63, 67, 72, 77, 83, 86, 88, 91, 92, 94, 104, 168, 169, 174
Wilmington, North Carolina, 28, 59, 60, 167, 181, 182, 183, 184, 199
Winnsboro, South Carolina, 77, 82, 88, 90, 91, 93, 94, 159, 165, 168, 177
Woodlands, Simm's plantation, 62, 111
Woods, Thomas J., 70, 95, 110, 119, 138, 146, 158

ENDNOTES

[1] Supplemental Report of the Joint Committee on the Conduct of the War, in two volumes; supplemental to Senate Report No. 142, 38th Congress, 2d session (Washington: Government Printing Office, 1866), 320. Also, William T. Sherman, Story of the Grand March. Major-General Sherman's Reports, (New York: Beadle and Company: Publishing date not visible), 41. https://ia700406.us.archive.org/14/items/majorgeneralsher00sher/majorgeneralsher00sher.pdf).

[2] James G. Gibbes, Who Burnt Columbia? (Newberry, South Carolina: Elbert H. Aull Company, 1902), 109.

[3] William Tecumseh Sherman, The Memoirs of General W.T. Sherman: All Volumes, January 21, 1875 in St. Louis. Memoirs of General William T. Sherman by Himself in two volumes (New York: D. Appleton and Co., 1875. Amazon Digital Services: Aceron Press, 2012) 10,115. Also, Sherman, Letter to his brother, May 12, 1862 http://politicalquotes.org/taxonomy/term/3672.

[4] Sherman's Memoirs, 9,182.

[5] Ibid., 9,441. Sherman gave notice of his intent to wage war against civilians in a letter that he wrote on September 4, 1864, to General Henry W. Halleck, headquartered in Washington as chief of staff for General Grant, who had been promoted to general-in-chief.

[6] Ibid., 9,187.

[7] Ibid., 10,234-10,268. Headquarters Military Division of the Mississippi, In the Field, Kingston, Georgia, November 9, 1864 *Special Field Orders, No. 120, November 9, 1864*

1. For the purpose of military operations, this army is divided into two wings viz.: The right wing, Major-General O. O. Howard commanding, composed of the Fifteenth and Seventeenth Corps; the left wing, Major-General H. W. Slocum commanding, composed of the Fourteenth and Twentieth Corps.

2. The habitual order of march will be, wherever practicable, by four roads, as nearly parallel as possible, and converging at points hereafter to be indicated in orders. The cavalry, Brigadier -

General Kilpatrick commanding, will receive special orders from the commander-in-chief.

3. There will be no general train of supplies, but each corps will have its ammunition-train and provision-train, distributed habitually as follows: Behind each regiment should follow one wagon and one ambulance; behind each brigade should follow a due proportion of ammunition - wagons, provision-wagons, and ambulances. In case of danger, each corps commander should change this order of march, by having his advance and rear brigades unencumbered by wheels. The separate columns will start habitually at 7 a.m., and make about fifteen miles per day, unless otherwise fixed in orders.

4. The army will forage liberally on the country during the march. To this end, each brigade commander will organize a good and sufficient foraging party, under the command of one or more discreet officers, who will gather, near the route traveled, corn or forage of any kind, meat of any kind, vegetables, corn-meal, or whatever is needed by the command, aiming at all times to keep in the wagons at least ten day's provisions for the command and three days' forage. Soldiers must not enter the dwellings of the inhabitants, or commit any trespass, but during a halt or a camp they may be permitted to gather turnips, potatoes, and other vegetables, and to drive in stock of their camp. To regular foraging parties must be instructed the gathering of provisions and forage at any distance from the road traveled.

5. To army corps commanders alone is intrusted the power to destroy mills, houses, cotton-gins, &c., and for them this general principle is laid down: In districts and neighborhoods where the army is unmolested no destruction of such property should be permitted; but should guerrillas or bushwhackers molest our march, or should the inhabitants burn bridges, obstruct roads, or otherwise manifest local hostility, then army commanders should order and enforce a devastation more or less relentless according to the measure of such hostility.

6. As for horses, mules, wagons, &c., belonging to the inhabitants, the cavalry and artillery may appropriate freely and without limit,

discriminating, however, between the rich, who are usually hostile, and the poor or industrious, usually neutral or friendly. Foraging parties may also take mules or horses to replace the jaded animals of their trains, or to serve as pack-mules for the regiments or bridges. In all foraging, of whatever kind, the parties engaged will refrain from abusive or threatening language, and may, where the officer in command thinks proper, give written certificates of the facts, but no receipts, and they will endeavor to leave with each family a reasonable portion for their maintenance.
7. Negroes who are able-bodied and can be of service to the several columns may be taken along, but each army commander will bear in mind that the question of supplies is a very important one and that his first duty is to see to them who bear arms.
8. The organization, at once, of a good pioneer battalion for each army corps, composed if possible of negroes, should be attended to. This battalion should follow the advance-guard, repair roads and double them if possible, so that the columns will not be delayed after reaching bad places. Also, army commanders should practice the habit of giving the artillery and wagons the road, marching their troops on one side, and instruct their troops to assist wagons at steep hills or bad crossings of streams.
9. Captain O.M. Poe, chief-engineer, will assign to each wing of the army a pontoon-train, fully equipped and organized; and the commanders thereof will see to their being properly protected at all times. By order of Major-General William T. Sherman
[8] Ibid., 10,233.
[9] Ibid.
[10] William Gilmore Simms, The History of South Carolina from its first European discovery to its erection into a Republic with a supplementary book, bringing the narrative down to the Present Time, (New York: Redfield,1860), 300.
http://books.google.com/books?id=snO4jfOwJu4C&printsec=frontco ver&dq=William+gilmore+simms+history+of+south+carolina&hl=en &sa=X&ei=jUeCU5n5GsTnsATp_IHICg&ved=0CC0Q6AEwAA#v= onepage&q=William%20gilmore%20simms%20history%20of%20so uth%20carolina&f=false

[11] Sherman's Memoirs, 10,224.

[12] Ibid., 10,223.

[13] Ibid., 10,233.

[14] Ibid.

[15] Gibbes,110.

[16] Ibid.

[17] Sherman's Memoirs, 11,672.

[18] General Sherman's Official Account of His Great March Through Georgia and the Carolinas: From His Departure from Chattanooga to the Surrender of General Joseph E. Johnston and the Confederate Forces Under His Command. To which is Added, General Sherman's Evidence Before the Congressional Committee on the Conduct of the War; the Animadversions of Secretary Stanton and General Halleck: with a Defence of His Proceedings, Etc. (Google eBook) (New York: Bunce & Huntington, 1865), 83, 109. http://books.google.com/books?id=KQ8TAAAAYAAJ&printsec_frontcover&source=gbs_ge_summaryr&cad=0#v=onepage&q&f=false

[19] Sherman's Memoirs, 10,788. Also, Sherman's Official Report, 37, 87. https://ia700406.us.archive.org/14/items/majorgeneralsher00sher/majorgeneralsher00sher.pdf (accessed January 15, 2014.)

[20] George Ward Nichols, The Story of the Great March, From the Diary of a Staff Officers, (Bedford, Massachusetts: Applewood Books, 1865), 51. http://books.google.com/books?id=ZUfkERcTmrkC&pg=PA310&dq=the+story+of+the+great+march&hl=en&sa=X&ei=96jzU5DnA7jLsQS29IDIAg&ved=0CBwQ6AEwAA#v=onepage&q=the%20story%20of%20the%20great%20march&f=false

[21] Sherman's Memoirs, 11,184.

[22] Howard would become head of the Freedmen's Bureau after the war and the founder of Howard University in Washington, D.C.

[23] Sherman's Memoirs, 11,180, 11,181.

[24] Sherman's Official Report, 85.

[25] Ibid.

[26] Sherman's Official Report, 41.

[27] Inflation calculator http://www.davemanuel.com/inflation-calculator.php. The 1865 dollar is valued at $14.50 in today's money, which made the damage to the state of Georgia and its military resources that Sherman estimated at $100 million worth more than $1.4 billion in 2014 dollars, and the $20 million that he estimated in confiscated property "waste and destruction" would be worth more than $280 million in 2014 dollars.

[28] Sherman's Official Report, 87.

[29] Sherman, Letter to his brother, May 12, 1862, http://politicalquotes.org/taxonomy/term/3672.

[30] F.B. Long with Barbara Long, The Civil War Day by Day: An Almanac 1861-1865, (New York: Da Capo Press, 1971), 125, 138, 171.

[31] Ibid., 171.

[32] Patricia G. McNeely, Debra Reddin van Tuyll, Henry H. Schulte, Knights of the Quill: Confederate Correspondents and their Civil War Reporting (Purdue University Press, West Lafayette, Indiana, 2010), 60, 72, 74.

[33] Sherman's Memoirs, 10,233. (Sherman's Special Field Orders No. 120. November 9, 1864.)

[34] Gibbes, 60, 61.

[35] Sherman's Memoirs, 11,897. Also, National Archives http://www.archives.gov/legislative/guide/house/chapter-06-war-claims.html

[36] The committee had been established in the House of Representatives on November 13, 1794, to handle war claims, pensions, and private land claims.

[37] Under the umbrella of a new act that was passed on March 3, 1871, the Commissioners of Claims considered 22,298 Civil War claims between 1871 and 1873 seeking more than $60 million in damages. The Commissioners barred 5,250 of the claims, authorized payment of $4,636,229.75 in claims, and disallowed over $55 million. The Committee on War Claims was created in 1873 when the name of the Committee on Revolutionary Claims (1825-1873) was changed to the Committee on War Claims, and its jurisdiction expanded to

include "claims arising from any war in which the United States has been engaged." To take into consideration all petitions and matters or things touching claims and demands on the United States as shall be presented or shall or may come in question and be referred to them by the House, and to report their opinion thereon, together with such propositions for relief therein as to them shall seem expedient.

[38] Sherman's Memoirs, 11,458.

[39] Ibid, 11,226.

[40] Ibid., 9,182.

[41] Ibid., 9,345.

[42] Ibid., 9,357.

[43] Ibid., 9,368.

[44] Ibid., 9,370.

[45] Ibid., 9,380, 9,381.

[46] Ibid., 9,405.

[47] Ibid., 9,523.

[48] Ibid., 12,075.

[49] Ibid., 9,405.

[50] Ibid., 9,477.

[51] Ibid., 9,499.

[52] Ibid.

[53] Ibid., 9,511.

[54] Ibid., 9,523.

[55] Ibid., 9,441.

[56] Ibid., 9,321.

[57] Ibid.

[58] Ibid., 9,543.

[59] Ibid., 9,193.

[60] Ibid., 9,263.

[61] Ibid., 9,629.

[62] Ibid., 9,652.

[63] Ibid., 9,674.

[64] F.B. Long with Barbara Long, The Civil War Day by Day: An Almanac 1861-1865, (New York: Da Capo Press, 1971), 573.

[65] Sherman's Memoirs, 9,742.

[66] Long, 579.

[67] Sherman's Memoirs, 9,886.

[68] Ibid., 9,909.
[69] Ibid., 15,262.
[70] Ibid., 10,048.
[71] Ibid., 10,193.
[72] Ibid., 10,197.
[73] Ibid., 10,286.
[74] Ibid., 10,202.
[75] Ibid., 10,268.
[76] Ibid., 10,278.
[77] Ibid., 15,262.
[78] Ibid., 10,306.
[79] Ibid.
[80] Ibid., 11,113.
[81] Ibid, 11,114.
[82] Ibid.,11,113.
[83] Gibbes, 60-61.
[84] Sherman's Memoirs, 10,358.
[85] Gibbes, 60-61.
[86] Sherman's Memoirs, 10,370.
[87] Ibid.,10,428.
[88] Ibid.,10,486.
[89] Ibid.,10,498.
[90] Ibid., 10,486.
[91] Nichols, 57.
[92] Sherman's Memoirs, 10,497.
[93] Ibid., 10,532.
[94] W.D. Dodson, Joseph Wheeler, Campaigns of Wheeler and his Cavalry, 1862-1865: From Material Furnished by Gen. Joseph Wheeler to which is Added His Course and Graphic Account of the Santiago Campaign of 1898. Publishing under the Auspices of Wheeler's Confederate Cavalry Association and Ed. by W. D. Dodson, historian, Parts 1-2, Good ebook, (Atlanta: Hudgins Publishing Company, 1899), 337. http://books.google.com/books?id=SCsePSD3YeEC&dq=Gen.+Hampton+thus+introduced+a+new+method+of+cavalry+fighting&source=gbs_navlinks_s,

Also, William Gilmore Simms, The History of South Carolina From Its First European Discovery to Its Erection into a Republic, Carlisle, Massachusetts: Applewood Books, 1860), 295.

[95] Sherman's Memoirs, 10,532.
[96] Ibid.,10,565.
[97] Ibid, 11,517.
[98] Dodson, 301, 302.
[99] Ibid.
[100] Sherman's Memoirs, 11,476.
[101] Ibid, 11,476.
[102] Dodson, 301, 302.
[103] Sherman's Memoirs, 10,742.
[104] Ibid., 10,764.
[105] Ibid., 11,033.
[106] Ibid., 10,784.
[107] Ibid., 10,785.
[108] Ibid., 10,781.
[109] Ibid., 10,788.
[110] Ibid, 10,782.
[111] Ibid., 10,846.
[112] Ibid., 10,940.
[113] Ibid.,10,823.
[114] He was the United States Treasury agent for the Department of the South.
[115] Sherman's Memoirs, 11,236.
[116] Ibid.
[117] Ibid., 11,176.
[118] Ibid., 11,180.
[119] Ibid., 11,653.
[120] Gibbes, 42.
[121] Ibid.
[122] Sherman Reports, 34.
[123] Sherman's Memoirs, 10,981.
[124] Ibid., 10,981.
[125] Ibid., 11,367.
[126] Ibid., 11,299.
[127] Ibid.

[128] Ibid., 11,327.

[129] Ibid., 11,281.

[130] Ibid., 11,012.

[131] Ibid., 11,024.

[132] Ibid.

[133] Ibid, 11,517.

[134] Ibid., 11,539.

[135] Ibid.

[136] Ibid.

[137] Ibid.

[138] Ibid.

[139] Ibid.

[140] Theodore Rosengarten, New Views on the Burning of Columbia, Fifty-Sixth Annual Meeting Address (Columbia, S.C.: Caroliniana Society, University of South Carolina, *1996-97, The Board of Trustees of the University of South Carolina.* http://library.sc.edu/socar/uscs/1993/addr93.html

[141] Sherman's Memoirs, 10,790.

[142] Ibid,11,472-11,473.

[143] Ibid., 11,496.

[144] Ibid., 11,506.

[145] Ibid., 11,517.

[146] Ibid.

[147] Ibid., 11,584.

[148] Ibid.

[149] Ibid., 11,577-11,611. (Also see: Howard C. Westwood, Sherman Marched—and proclaimed "land for the landless," The Civil War in South Carolina: Selections from the South Carolina Historical Magazine, South Carolina Historical Magazine 85: 33-50, edited by Lawrence S. Rowland and Stephen G. Hoffius, (Charleston, S.C.: House House Press, 2011), 270.

[150] Westwood, 277-280.

[151] Ibid.

[152] Linda Malone, Fairfield Remembers Sherman, (Winnsboro, S.C.: Fairfield Archives and History, 2006), 126.

[153] Sherman's Memoirs, 11,434.

[154] Ibid., 11,405.

[155] Ibid., 11,773.

[156] Ibid., 11,402-11,403.

[157] Goldsboro was frequently spelled Goldsborough.

[158] Ibid.,11,402.

[159] Ibid., 11,642.

[160] William Gilmore Simms, The Sack and Destruction of the City of Columbia, S.C. to which is added A List of the Property Destroyed. (Columbia, S.C.: Power Press of Daily Phoenix, 1865), 9.

[161] Sherman's Memoirs,12,544.

[162] Ibid., 11,948.

[163] Ibid., 11,425.

[164] Gibbes, 65.

[165] Report of the Committee on the Destruction of Churches in the Diocese of South Carolina during the Late War presented to the Protestant Episcopal Convention May, 1868. (Charleston, S.C.: Walker, agt. Stationer and Printer, 1868), 2.

[166] Rosengarten.

[167] Dobson, 421.

[168] Sherman's Memoirs, 11,647.

[169] Ibid., 11,423.

[170] Ibid. 11,657.

[171] South Carolina Highway Historical Marker Guide, (S.C. Department of Archives and History, Columbia, S.C.,1998), 124-125. (about 1 mile south of Hampton at intersection of US 601 and Road 68 Marker 25-8.)

[172] Ibid., 22. It was originally built in 1757 but was burned during the Revolutionary War. It was rebuilt from the remaining walls in 1826, but was never rebuilt after being burned the second time during the Civil War. (On Road 21, 1.7 miles from intersection of 21 and U.S. 17 near Gardens Corner. Marker 7-4.)

[173] Report of the Committee on the Destruction of Churches, 4, 5.

[174] Ibid.

[175] The Columbia Record, March 21, 1936.

[176] Ibid.

[177] William Gilmore Simms, The Sack and Destruction of the City of Columbia, S.C. to which is added A List of the Property Destroyed. (Columbia, S.C.: Power Press of Daily Phoenix, 1865), 6.

[178] Sherman's Memoirs, 11,965.

[179] www.stmichaelschurch.net/about-us/history/bells
http://www.stmichaelschurch.net/about-us/history/bells/ At war's end, the Vestry reclaimed the metal and had the bells recast in London at the original foundry. The new frame was incorrectly installed by the local workmen, and the bells could not be rung. From 1868 until 1993 the bells were only chimed. After the 1989 hurricane, the Vestry again sent the bells back to London to the original foundry, now named The Whitechapel Bell Foundry Ltd., to have all the fittings replaced. A new wooden frame was fabricated and in 1993, the bells were returned to Charleston and rehung by Whitechapel, the original founders. Local ringers are now learning this ancient and uniquely Anglican art form and the bells again ring out over the city with the sounds of Change Ringing.
http://www.stmichaelschurch.net/about-us/history/bells/#sthash.1bPoV3Vl.dpuf Also, Report of the Committee on the Destruction of Churches, 9.

[180] Daniel L. Morrill, The Civil War in the Carolinas, (Nautical & Aviation Publishing Co. of America, 2002), 468.

[181] Ibid., 467-468.

[182] Sherman's Memoirs, 12,567.

[183] Ibid., 11,962.

[184] Ibid., 11,985.

[185] Ibid., 11,971.

[186] Ibid., 11,154

[187] Ibid.

[188] Nichols, 141.

[189] Ibid.,131. Also, Gibbes, 65-67.

[190] Sherman's Memoirs, 11,993.

[191] South Carolina Highway Historical Marker Guide, (S.C. Department of Archives and History, Columbia, S.C., 1998), 17. UDC marker at 5-1 at Rivers Bridge State Park at intersection of 449 and Hwy. 31, south of Bamberg.

[192] Sherman, 11,982.

[193] Sherman's soldiers passed through what is now Bamberg County in February 1865. Plantations in the area were burned, including

Simms' 4,000-acre plantation, Woodlands. Nearby landowners accused Isaac Nimmons of instigating the other enslaved blacks to burn the plantation. William Gilmore Simms, Jr. reported what happened: "Some time after the army had passed, a jury of citizens in the neighborhood arrested my father's coachman and body servant Isaac Nimmons and tried him for the burning of Woodlands. The weight of the evidence exonerated Isaac, although there was a good deal of feeling against him, but general opinion was that the dwelling was burnt by some of the bands of bummers that hung on to the outskirts of the army." http://www.sharedhistory.org/nimmons.aspx. Accessed April 9, 2014.

[194] Gibbes, 105.

[195] The Robertville Church was built in 1848 as an Episcopal church in Gillisonville and moved to Robertville by Black Swamp Baptists in 1871. South Carolina Historical Marker Guide, S.C. (Columbia, S.C.:Archives and History), 128, Robertville Baptist Church, Robertville, Marker 27-1.

[196] In modern day Jasper County.

[197] Sherman's Memoirs, 11,996.

[198] Ibid., S.C. Secondary Rd. 70 (Old Allendale Hwy.) just north of the Salkehatchie River Bridge. Marker 6-5.

[199] South Carolina Historical Marker Guide, 20. (Intersection of S.C. Hwy. 3 and Main St., Blackville. Marker 6-5).

[200] South Carolina Historical Marker Guide, 20. (S.C. Secondary Rd. 70 (old Allendale Hwy.) just north of the Salkehatchie River Bridge.)

[201] South Carolina Historical Marker Guide, S.C. Archives and History, 131. (The marker is located on the east side of SC 462 at the church in Gillisonville Marker 27-23.)

[202] Sherman's Memoirs, 12,000.

[203] Nichols, 139, 144.

[204] Simms, 8.

[205] Nichols, 146.

[206] Dan L. Morrill, The Civil War in the Carolinas, The Nautical & Aviation Publishing Company of America, Charleston, South Carolina, 2002), 464, 470. Also Private Mary Chesnut, 227.

[207] South Carolina Highway Historical Marker Guide, 187. Marker 404.

[208] Ibid.

[209] R.N. Scott, ed., The War of the Rebellion—A Compilation of the Official Records of the Union and Confederate Armies, Series I, Vol. 47, part one. (Washington, D.C.: Government Printing Office, 1885), 858-59, 866, 878-80, 881-82-891-92.

[210] Sherman, 12,018.

[211] Morrill, 466.

[212] Marble Marker, northwest corner of intersection of US 78 (Richland Street) and U.S. 1 (York Street) in Aiken. It is in the extreme southeastern corner of the First Baptist Churchyard, ten feet north of Richland Street.

[213] South Carolina Highway Historical Marker Guide, 177, marker 38-3, Orangeburg. The South Carolina Canal and Rail Road track from Charleston to Hamburg (across from Augusta) was finished on December 25, 1830, and by 1833 its 136 miles made it the world's longest railroad.

[214] Nichols, 149.

[215] Simms, 7.

[216] Sherman, 12,025.

[217] South Carolina Highway Historical Marker Guide, 178. (Edisto Gardens, Orangeburg, Marker 38-5.)

[218] Sherman, 12,037.

[219] Ibid., 12,023. The home was built in 1846.

[220] At 525 Whitman Street.

[221] South Carolina Highway Historical Marker Guide, 178.

[222] Ibid.

[223] Sherman, 12,054.

[224] Nichols, 154.

[225] Ibid., 9,523.

[226] Ibid., 12,075.

[227] Nichols, 156.

[228] Sherman, 12,042.

[229] Simms, 9.

[230] Ibid.

[231] Ibid.

[232] Selby, 178.

[233] Simms, 10, and Thomas J. Goodwyn, letter written June 8, 1866 in Calhoun County to Rev. Colin Campbell Murchison while Goodwyn was at his plantation at Fort Motte. Courtesy of Goodwyn's great-granddaughter Caroline Legare Judson.

[234] Goodwyn letter.

[235] Conyngham, 326.

[236] Six stars mark spots where the State House was hit.

[237] Michael Trinkley, Factory Cemetery, Lexington County, South Carolina, Chicora Research Contribution 340, prepared for Greg Lehman, (Columbia, S.C.: The Mungo Company, Irmo, Chicora Foundation), 2001.

[238] Nichols, 157.

[239] Nichols, 159.

[240] Nichols, 158.

[241] Simms, 11.

[242] Long, 638.

[243] Long, 640.

[244] South Carolina Highway Historical Marker Guide, 152. (Near Red Bank Creek, Lexington vicinity. Marker 32-27.)

[245] Ibid.

[246] South Carolina Historical Marker Guide, 151. (Corner of Butler and Church streets, Lexington, Located at the corner of Butler and Church Streets in downtown Lexington, the church at the present site became the fourth on the site in 1958. Marker 43-24.)

[247] Joseph Conte, Autobiography, (http://docsouth.unc.edu/fpn/leconte/leconte.html, University Library, The University of North Carolina at Chapel Hill, 2004), 205.

[248] Ibid.

[249] Ibid.

[250] Sherman's Memoirs, 12,057.

[251] LeConte, 207.

[252] Sherman's Memoirs, 12,061.

[253] Ibid., 147. (Marker 32-5.)

[254] Gibbes, 6.

[255] Sherman, 12,081.

[256] Simms, 10.

[257] Sherman's Memoirs, 12,072, 12,069.

[258] Goodwyn letter.

[259] Gibbes, 5.

[260] South Carolina Historical Marker Guide, South Carolina Archives and History, 90. (In front of the Century House on Railroad Ave., Ridgeway. Marker 20-1)

[261] Nichols, 156.

[262] Wheeler, 327.

[263] Ibid., 826

[264] Ibid., 327.

[265] Edwin J. Scott, 69. Conyngham, 337.

[266] Sherman's Memoirs, 12,081.

[267] On Friday, February 17, 1865. South Carolina Historical Marker Guide, 147. (US 378, West Columbia, Marker 32-3. Incorporated in 1834, it was rebuilt and operated after the war.)

[268] Conyngham, 325.

[269] Sherman said Alston was 15 miles north of Columbia, but by today's maps it is 25 miles.

[270] Official Records, Series 1, vol. 47/1:21, 22.

[271] http://dobrinkman.net/bridge/1865.htm

[272] Nichols, 161.

[273] *The State,* February 18, 1918.

[274] Simms,12.

[275] Goodwyn letter.

[276] Ibid., 12.

[277] Wheeler, 333, 334.

[278] Wheeler, 328.

[279] Simms, 11.

[280] Goodwyn letter.

[281] Gibbes, 47.

[282] Goodwyn letter. Conyngham thought there were three aldermen, but Goodwyn mentioned only one in his letter.

[283] Conyngham, 327.

[284] Goodwyn letter.

[285] Sherman's Memoirs. 12,069, 12,072.

[286] Conyngham, 327.

[287] Sherman's Memoirs, 12,092.

[288] Ibid., 12,091.

[289] Simms, 11.

[290] Sherman, 12,056.

[291] Simms, 11, Wheeler, 329.

[292] Wheeler, 329.

[293] Gibbes, 47.

[294] Ibid., 46.

[295] Ibid., 50.

[296] Goodwyn.

[297] Simms, 14.

[298] *Chicago Tribune,* January, 1873, *The State,* February 18, 1918, *The Columbia Record*, March 21, 1936.

[299] Gibbes, 30.

[300] *The State,* February 18, 1918.

[301] Ibid., and *The Columbia Record,* March 21, 1936.

[302] *The State,* February 18, 1918.

[303] Ibid.

[304] Simms, 14.

[305] Ibid., 16.

[306] Goodwyn.

[307] Simms, 14.

[308] *The State,* February 18, 1918.

[309] *The State,* March 21, 1936. The Rev. Peter Shand, letter to Mrs. Howard Kennedy, Hagerstown, Md., written in Columbia, S.C., March 9, 1868 and published in The State, March 21, 1936. *The State's* copy of the letter came to it in 1930 from Dr. Yates Snowden, professor of history at the University of South Carolina, to whom it had been given by the Rev. Mr. Shand's grandson, Dr. Robert Wilson of Charleston, dean of the Medical College of the State of South Carolina.

[310] Helen Kohn Hennig, Columbia Capital City of South Carolina 1786-1936, (Columbia, S.C: R.L. Bryan Company, 1936), 9. All the streets were 100 feet wide except for six, which were 150 feet wide.

[311] Ibid.

[312] Shand, *The State*, March 21, 1936.

[313] Simms, 14.

[314] Gibbes, 95.

[315] Ibid.

[316] Simms, 14.
[317] Oliver Otis Howard, Autobiography of Oliver Otis Howard, Vol. 2, (Baker and Taylor Company, New York, 1907),1,867.
[318] Conyngham, 328.
[319] Sherman's Memoirs, 12,104.
[320] Ibid., 12,104.
[321] Gibbes, 101.
[322] Howard, 1,867, Gibbes, 22.
[323] Sherman's Memoirs, 12,119.
[324] Howard, 1,867.
[325] Gibbes, 27.
[326] Ibid., 133.
[327] Simms, 16.
[328] Sherman's Memoirs, 12,104.
[329] Ibid., 12,107.
[330] Ibid., 12119.
[331] Ibid., 12,115.
[332] Simms, 17.
[333] Ibid.
[334] Goodwyn.
[335] Sherman's Memoirs, 12,126.
[336] Ibid., 12,126.
[337] Ibid., 12,161, 12,162.
[338] Ibid., 12,172.
[339] Goodwyn.
[340] Ibid., 12,188.
[341] South Carolina Confederate Relic Room and Military Museum; Also, Columbia City Directory 1899.
[342] South Carolina Confederate Relic Room and Military Museum.
[343] Simms, 53.
[344] Ibid.
[345] Ibid.
[346] Gibbes, 131.
[347] Goodwyn.
[348] Gibbes, 132.
[349] Ibid.
[350] Simms, 53.

[351] William Gilmore Simms and Mary C. Simms Oliphant, The History of South Carolina, (Columbia, S.C.: The State Company, 1912), Simms History, 303.

[352] Goodwyn.

[353] Gibbes, 13.

[354] Gibbes, 13.

[355] Le Conte. Joseph LeConte, 1823-1901 and William Dallam Armes, b. 1860, The Autobiography of Joseph LeConte. (New York: D. Appleton and Company, 1903), http://docsouth.unc.edu/fpn/leconte/menu.html

[356] Gibbes, 32.

[357] Goodwyn.

[358] Gibbes, 135.

[359] Gibbes, 22.

[360] The Columbia Record, March 21, 1936.

[361] Simms, 17.

[362] Simms History, 303.

[363] Gibbes, 132.

[364] Simms History, 303.

[365] William Gilmore Simms and Mary C. Simms Oliphant, The History of South Carolina, (Columbia, S.C.: The State Company, 1912), 305.

[366] Sherman's Memoirs, 12,198.

[367] Ibid.

[368] Ibid.

[369] Ibid.

[370] Ibid., 12, 201.

[371] Simms, 15. Although Simms was told the officer was a major, it is likely that the "editor from Detroit" was General Alpheus Starkey Williams, who was known to own a newspaper in Detroit.

[372] Gibbes, 39.

[373] Simms, 15.

[374] Ibid.

[375] Gibbes, 134.

[376] Possibly General Perry "Powhatan" Carter.

[377] Gibbes, 135.

[378] Gibbes, 18.

[379] Ibid., 19.

[380] Ibid., 135.

[381] Simms, 38.

[382] Nell S. Graydon, Tales of Columbia, (R.L. Bryan Company, Columbia, S.C., 1981), 46.

[383] South Carolina Highway Historical Marker Guide, 190. (Marker 40-17)

[384] Michael Trinkley, Factory Cemetery, Lexington County, South Carolina, Chicora Research Contribution 340, prepared for Greg Lehman, (Columbia, S.C.: The Mungo Company, Irmo, Chicora Foundation), 2001. "There are some accounts suggesting that James Gibbes' neighbors and friends were shocked at his profiteering. Before Gibbes sold the mill, he was not only profiting from the mill and his factory, but also from selling luxury items which made it through the Union naval blockade. It is likely that resentment ran high, but Dr. Robert Gibbes characterized the criticisms as "unjust, unkind, and un-Christian attacks," and justified the high prices by noting how much more he could obtain from the European market—hardly a comment likely to salve many feelings. It was probably that wave of war-time resentment that encouraged them to sell the mill to Colonel L.D. Childs of Lincolnton, North Carolina in 1862. Childs paid $100,000 (probably in Confederate bills) for the mill. James Gibbes also sold Childs 800 bales of cotton at 17¢ a pound and agreed to serve as the agent for the mill's products, selling them in his Columbia stores. Within six months, the price of manufactured goods increased from 500 to 2,200 per cent. Yarns which sold for $1.25 brought $10." But the prosperity of the mill's owner and its agent were not to last long.

[385] Ibid.

[386] Gibbes, 19.

[387] Ibid., 21.

[388] Simms, 17.

[389] Gibbes, 15, 16. Part 1st; General Depositions of Wm. Tecumseh Sherman, General of the Army of the United States, and Gen. O.O. Howard, U.S.A. for the Defence, and letters from some of the depositions for the claimants filed in certain Claims vs. United States, pending before the Mixed Commission on British and American

Claims, in Washington, D.C., Charleston, S.C. Walker, Evans & Cogswell, 1878).

[390] Simms, 18.

[391] Ibid.

[392] Ibid.

[393] Ibid., 36.

[394] Ibid., 20.

[395] Ibid., 23.

[396] Ibid., 21.

[397] South Carolina Highway Historical Marker Guide, 190. (Marker 409 Ebenezer was rebuilt in 1870.)

[398] The convention had been moved to Charleston after a smallpox outbreak was reported in Columbia.

[399] South Carolina Highway Historical Marker Guide, 190. (Marker 40-17)

[400] The church had originally been built in 1811 on the Sumter Street corner, where the First Baptist Church had first stood. It had been converted to a Methodist Church when the Baptist church was built at 1306 Hampton street.

[401] Simms, 15.

[402] Shand, *The State,* March 21, 1936.

[403] Simms, 15.

[404] Report of the Committee on the Destruction of Churches, 14. St. Peter's has a record of a flagon (decanter) that was stolen by a Union soldier during the Civil War and returned in 1944 by his family.[369]

[405] Simms, 33.

[406] Ibid., 19.

[407] Ibid., 24.

[408] *The Columbia Record*, South Carolina, July 13, 1963.

[409] South Carolina College was chartered in 1801 and opened in 1805.

[410] After the war, the Leconte family moved to California where Dr. Leconte became a professor at the newly founded USC at Berkeley. Leconte was a co-founder with John Muir of the Sierra Club.

[411] LeConte, 32, 33.

[412] Ibid., (http://docsouth.unc.edu/fpn/leconte/leconte.html Last updated February 13, 2014), 227.

[413] Simms, 42, 43.

[414] LeConte 227. Also, South Carolina Highway Historical Marker Guide, 191. (Marker 40-27)

[415] *The State*, March 21, 1936.

[416] Gibbes, 133, 134.

[417] Ibid.

[418] Howard, 1,867.

[419] Gibbes, 38.

[420] Shand, *The State,* March 21, 1936.

[421] Gibbes, 10.

[422] Simms, 43.

[423] Official Records, Vol. 47/1:272-273, 310, 529.

[424] Simms, 43.

[425] Ibid.

[426] Ibid.

[427] Ibid.

[428] *The Columbia Record,* March 21, 1936.

[429] Gibbes, 133, 134.

[430] Goodwyn.

[431] Simms, 24.

[432] Frank F. Whilden, Columbia Burned 67 Years Ago today," *The State,* Columbia, S.C., February 17, 1932.

[433] Gibbes, 28.

[434] Howard, 1,881.

[435] Simms, 19.

[436] Ibid.

[437] Sherman's Memoirs, 12,219.

[438] Goodwyn.

[439] Ibid.

[440] Goodwyn letter to Governor Magrath, February 26, 1865. Courtesy of Goodwyn's great-granddaughter Caroline LeGare Judson.

[441] Gibbes, 47.

[442] Gibbes, 91.

[443] Following the Civil War and the destruction of his Columbia home, Goodwyn and his family lived in Fort Motte, S.C. http://184.168.105.185/archivegrid/collection/data/535721834

[444] Gibbes, 55.

[445] Shand, *The State.*

[446] Ibid.
[447] Ibid.
[448] Gibbes, 62.
[449] Ibid.
[450] Conyngham, 380.
[451] Ibid.
[452] Ibid.
[453] Sherman's Memoirs,12,219.
[454] Ibid., 12,807.
[455] Ibid., 12,213.
[456] Ibid.
[457] Gibbes, 16.
[458] SERCO, Lower Richland Heritage Corridor Visitor's Guide, Southeast Rural Community Outreach, 2012.
[459] Listed in the National Register March 27, 1986. The plantation was purchased in 1858 by Edward Barnwell Heyward, a close friend of James and Mary Boykin Chesnut, who lived nearby on the Mulberry Plantation near Camden. President Jefferson Davis was an unexpected visitor during the Civil War when his train was running late near Kingston, 10 miles from the plantation. Davis, who was afraid his horse would break a leg in the dark, stopped to spend the night at the Heyward house. As many as 976 slaves were living at Goodwill during the war and hundreds more were sent from another plantation near the Combahee river. Owned today by Larry Faulkenberry, the plantation has a frame mill building (ca. 1857-1870), two slave cabins (ca. 1858), a blacksmith shop built after the Civil War, and a main house that was built in the late nineteenth century. Goodwill also contains a carriage house, tenant house, barn and corn crib and a once-working still with a few gallons of moonshine.
[460] South Carolina Highway Historical Marker Guide, 188. (Marker 40-12)
[461] Sherman's Memoirs, 12,232.
[462] South Carolina Highway Historical Marker Guide, 188. (Marker 40-13)
[463] Sherman, 12,232.

[464] William Gilmore Simms, The Sack and Destruction of Columbia, S.C., 3.

[465] Rosengarten.

[466] Simms, 55.

[467] Ibid., 54.

[468] Ibid.

[469] Ibid.

[470] Ibid., 5.

[471] Joseph LeConte, 1823-1901 and William Dallam Armes, b. 1860. The Autobiography of Joseph LeConte New York: D. Appleton and Company, 1903), 225.

[472] LeConte, 37-42.

[473] Gibbes, 55.

[474] Official Records, Series 1, Vol. 47, 1: 21, 22, 40, 41.

[475] Ibid.

[476] Shand, *The State,* March 21, 1936.

[477] Ibid.

[478] Edwin J. Scott, Random Recollections of a Long Life, 1806 to 1876, (Columbia, S.C.: Charles A. Calvo. Jr., 1884).

[479] Gibbes, 44.

[480] Gibbes, 40.

[481] Ibid.

[482] *The Columbia Record,* March 21, 1936.

[483] *New York Times,* September 15, 1873.

[484] Gibbes, 41.

[485] Gibbes, 16.

[486] Morrill, 477. Also, Alfred Roman, The military operations of General Beauregard in the War between the States, 1861 to 1865, including a brief personal sketch and a narrative of his services in the war with Mexico, 1846-8 in two volumes, (New York: Harper Brothers 1884), 643. http://books.google.com/books?id=nWwDAAAAYAAJ&printsec=frontcover&dq=general+beauregard&hl=en&sa=X&ei=HkH6U6v3OPPKsQTTr4CACw&ved=0CCUQ6AEwAQ#v=onepage&q=general%20beauregard&f=false

[487] Deposition of Sherman, December 11, 1872 (Mixed Commission, XIV, 91; March 30, 1872, Mixed Commission, III,) 12.

[488] Rosengarten. http://library.sc.edu/socar/uscs/1993/addr93.html

[489] Deposition of Sherman, December 11, 1872; Mixed Commission, XIV, 91; March 30, 1872, Mixed Commission, III, 12; Rachel Sherman Thorndike, ed., The Sherman Letters: Correspondence between General and Senator Sherman from 1837 to 1891, 266.

[490] Gibbes, 109.

[491] Ibid., 16.

[492] Ibid.

[493] Ibid., 15.

[494] Ibid., 16.

[495] Ibid.,17.

[496] Ibid.

[497] Ibid.

[498] Sherman's Memoirs, 12,235.

[499] South Carolina historical marker guide, 90. (SC 213, 1.5 miles from its intersection with SC 215 near Jenkinsville, Marker 20-22.)

[500] Gibbes, 60, 61.

[501] http://www.measuringworth.com/uscompare/relativevalue.php.

[502] Gibbes, 60, 61.

[503] Ibid.

[504] Jamieson was known as "The Father of The Citadel" because of legislation he introduced to establish a military school in Charleston.

[505] John Witherspoon DuBose, General Joseph Wheeler and the Army of Tennessee, (New York: Neale Publishing Company, 1912), 436.

[506] Ibid.

[507] Ibid., 437.

[508] Ibid., 438.

[509] Official Records, Ser. 1, XLVII, 2: 596, 597.

[510] Ibid.

[511] Sherman's Memoirs, 12,172.

[512] Malone, 136.

[513] Ibid., 135, 136.

[514] Sherman's Memoirs, 12,202.

[515] Ibid., 12,236.

[516] Ibid.

[517] Malone, 136.
[518] DuBose, 435.
[519] Ibid.
[520] Ibid.
[521] Sherman's Memoirs, 12,292.
[522] Morrill, 477.
[523] South Carolina Historical Marker Guide, 144. (Road 39, about 1.3 mi. N from I-20 near Cypress Crossroads. Marker 31-6).
[524] Ibid., 72. (Marker 16-13)
[525] Ibid., 58
[526] Ginger Morton http://www.jamesjenkins.net/chesterfield/busdistnorth/203emain.html
[527] LeConte, 50.
[528] Ibid., 50, 51.
[529] South Carolina Highway Historical Marker Guide, 157. (US 76, about 8 miles w of Marion at Pee Dee River Bridge. Marker 34-2.)
[530] Patricia G. McNeely, Debra Reddin van Tuyll, Henry H. Schulte, Knights of the Quill, Confederate Correspondents and their Civil War Reporting, (West Lafayette, Indiana: Purdue University Press, 2010), 174.
[531] Ibid.
[532] Sherman's Memoirs, 12,269.
[533] South Carolina Highway Historical Marker Guide, 167. (Marker 35-23)
[534] Sherman's Memoirs, 12,280.
[535] Ibid., 12,283.
[536] Ibid., 12,292.
[537] Ibid.
[538] South Carolina Highway Historical Marker Guide, 71, (Road 49, about 0.5 miles from U.S 52, south of Darlington).
[539] McNeely, 174.
[540] South Carolina Highway Historical Marker Guide, 144 (Road 7, 6.4 mi. west of Manville at Spring Hill in Lee County).
[541] S.C. Highway Historical Marker Guide, 133. (Marker 28-6.)
[542] Sherman's Memoirs, 12,308.
[543] Ibid., 12,331.
[544] Ibid, 12,320.

[545] Ibid., 12,364.
[546] Ibid.
[547] Ibid., 12,375.
[548] Ibid., 12,387.
[549] Ibid., 12,410.
[550] Ibid., 12,382.
[551] Ibid., 12,410.
[552] Ibid., 12,405.
[553] Ibid.
[554] Ibid., 12,393.
[555] Ibid., 12,439.
[556] Ibid., 12,474.
[557] Ibid., 12,251.
[558] Ibid., 12,647.
[559] Ibid., 12,671.
[560] Ibid., 12, 486.
[561] Ibid., 12,531.
[562] Ibid., 12,706.
[563] Ibid., 12,762.
[564] Ibid.
[565] Ibid., 12,910.
[566] Ibid., 12,922.
[567] Ibid., 12,934.
[568] Ibid.
[569] Ibid., 12,946.
[570] Ibid.
[571] Ibid.
[572] Ibid., 12,957.
[573] Ibid.
[574] Ibid., 12,807.
[575] Ibid., 12,545, 12,546.
[576] Ibid., 12,546.
[577] Ibid., 13,162.
[578] Ibid., 13,185.
[579] Ibid., 12,823.
[580] Ibid., 13,220.
[581] Ibid., 13,244.

[582] Ibid.

[583] Ibid., 13,268.

[584] Ibid., 13,361.

[585] Ibid., 13,280.

[586] Ibid., 13,543.

[587] Ibid., 13,292.

[588] Ibid., 13,511.

[589] Ibid., 13,372.

[590] Ibid., 13,315.

[591] Ibid., 13,556.

[592] Ibid.

[593] Ibid., 13,429.

[594] Ibid., 13,533.

[595] Ibid., 13,591.

[596] Ibid.

[597] Ibid.

[598] Ibid., 13,603.

[599] Ibid.

[600] Ibid., 13,680.

[601] Ibid., 13,691.

[602] Ibid., 13,680.

[603] Ibid., 13,690.

[604] Ibid., 13,702.

[605] Ibid.

[606] Ibid.

[607] Ibid., 13,726.

[608] Ibid., 15,262.

[609] Ibid., 13,636.

[610] Ibid., 13,635.

[611] Ibid., 13,738.

[612] Ibid., 13,749.

[613] Ibid.,13,772.

[614] Ibid., 13,784.

ABOUT THE AUTHOR

Patricia G. "Pat" McNeely is Professor Emerita at the University of South Carolina in Columbia, South Carolina, where she taught reporting for 33 years in the School of Journalism. Before joining the USC faculty, she was a reporter and editor for The State, The Columbia Record and The Greenville News. She is co-author of Knights of the Quill: Confederate Correspondents and their Civil War Reporting, and author of Fighting Words: A Media History of South Carolina and Palmetto Press: The History of South Carolina's Newspapers, which will be reissued in 2015.

Made in the USA
Charleston, SC
11 January 2015